Her Blue Body
Everything We Know

ALSO BY ALICE WALKER

FICTION
Now Is the Time to Open Your Heart
The Way Forward Is with a Broken Heart
You Can't Keep a Good Woman Down
The Third Life of Grange Copeland
Meridian
In Love & Trouble
The Color Purple
The Temple of My Familiar
Possessing the Secret of Joy
By the Light of My Father's Smile

NONFICTION
Anything We Love Can Be Saved
In Search of Our Mothers' Gardens
Living by the Word
Warrior Marks (with Pratibha Parmar)
The Same River Twice: Honoring the Difficult

POETRY
A Poem Traveled Down My Arm: Poems and Drawings
Absolute Trust in the Goodness of the Earth
Horses Make a Landscape Look More Beautiful
Revolutionary Petunias
Once
Good Night Willie Lee, I'll See You in the Morning

BOOKS FOR CHILDREN
To Hell with Dying
Langston Hughes, American Poet
Finding the Green Stone

EDITED BY ALICE WALKER
I Love Myself When I Am Laughing:
A Zora Neale Hurston Reader

Alice Walker

Her Blue Body Everything We Know

EARTHLING POEMS 1965-1990
COMPLETE

A HARVEST BOOK
HARCOURT, INC.
Orlando   Austin   New York   San Diego   Toronto   London

www.HarcourtBooks.com

*Permissions for material used in this book can be found on page 463,
which constitutes a continuation of the copyright page.*

ISBN 0-15-602861-1

The Library of Congress has cataloged the paperback edition as follows:

Walker, Alice, 1944–
Her blue body everything we know: earthling poems, 1965-1990
Complete/Alice Walker.—1st ed.
p.   cm.
ISBN 0-15-140040-7
ISBN 0-15-640093-6 (pbk.)
I. Title
PS3573.A425H47   1991   90-5160
811'.54—dc20

Printed in the United States of America

A C E G I K J H F D B

*This book was printed on acid-free recycled content paper,
containing more than 10 percent postconsumer waste.*

Always to You
Beautiful One
From whom
I have come.
And to whom
I shall happily
Return.

Contents

Preface

It surprises me to see I have been writing and publishing poetry for twenty-five years. For which I have Poetry itself to thank. Because I was so often filled with despair over my own and the world's shortcomings, especially during childhood, adolescence, and young adulthood, I assumed I would be a suicide by the age of thirty.

Not so, I am happy to report. Out of the gloom that covered me rose Poetry, again and again, on its charger of sunlight. My life has been saved more times than I can count by this bright, unbeckoned stranger from my own deepest ocean and farthest shore.

Pay attention, it has said, there is in *you* the green tree you see from your rope. There is in *you* the strong river in which you would drown. There is in *you* the heart you are missing in your sister and fellow beings.

I have climbed back into life over and over on a ladder made of words, but knitted, truly, by the Unknowable. Through Poetry I have lived to find within myself my own "invincible sun."

In keeping faith with Poetry's honest help to me, I have not deleted or changed—beyond a word or two—anything

I have written, though greatly tempted at times to do so. The young self, the naive promiscuous self, the ill or self-destructive self, the angry and hurt self, appear doubly vulnerable now, in light of my unexpected bonus of years, and the experience they have brought me. I embrace them all, as Poetry has embraced me. The poem, the world and I (and you) are one. It is at the point that we meet that you hold this book.

Out of Unknowing
and Sacrifice
we come
bearing our wonders
our wounds
and our gifts.

Once

There were palm trees
   palmed
   against
   the sky

and warthogs
waving flags.

        This is one of several poems
I did not include in my first collection of poetry, *Once*. It
remains an enduring "snapshot" of East Africa the summer
of 1965 when I traveled there and where, in Kenya, I helped
construct a school. All of the poems in *Once* were written
in Africa, while sitting underneath a tree facing Mount
Kenya, or at Sarah Lawrence College in New York, where
I was completing my senior year. It was often necessary to
leave my belongings in the care of relatives and friends
while I traveled. It was in this way that I lost the small blue
notebook that contained the above poem and others, which,
unfortunately, I do not recall verbatim. There *is* a poem
from this period that I wrote when a friend pointed out to

me that I could not call the first section "African Images, Glimpses from a Tiger's Back," because, he said, "There are no tigers in Africa!"

There are no tigers
in Africa!
You say.
Frowning.
Yes. I say.
Smiling.
But they are
very beautiful.

For Howard Zinn

Poverty was not a calamity for me. It was always balanced by the richness of light . . . circumstances helped me. To correct a natural indifference I was placed halfway between misery and the sun. Misery kept me from believing that all was well under the sun, and the sun taught me that history wasn't everything.

—ALBERT CAMUS, *De L'Envers et l'endroit*

I found in myself an invincible sun.

Ibid.

AFRICAN IMAGES
Glimpses from a Tiger's Back

Beads around
my neck
Mt. Kenya away
over pineappled hills
Kikuyuland.

A book of poems
Mt. Kenya's
Bluish peaks
"Wangari!"*
My new name.

*Kikuyu clan name indicating honorary acceptance into the Leopard clan.

A green copse
And hovering
Quivering
Near our bus
A shy gazelle.

morning mists
On the road
an Elephant
He knows
his rights.

A strange noise!
"Perhaps an elephant
is eating our roof?"
In the morning
much blue.

A tall warrior
and at his feet
only
Elephant bones.

Elephant legs
In a store
To hold
Umbrellas.

A young man
Puts a question
In his language
I invariably
End up
Married.

The clear Nile
A fat crocodile
Scratches his belly
And yawns.

The rain forest
Red orchids—glorious!
And near one's eyes
The spinning cobra.

A small boat
A placid lake
Suddenly at one's hand
Two ears—
Hippopotamus.

An ocean of grass
A sea of sunshine
And near my hand
Water buffalo.

See! through the trees!
A leopard in
the branches—
No, only a giraffe
Munching his dinner.

Fast rapids
Far below
Begins
The lazy Nile.

A silent lake
Bone strewn banks
Luminous
In the sun.

Uganda mountains
Black soil
White snow
And in the valley
Zebra.

African mornings
Are not for sleeping
In the early noon
The servant, John,
comes
To wake me.

Very American
I want to eat
The native food—
But a whole goat!

Holding three fingers
The African child
Looked up at me
The sky was very
Blue.

In the dance
I see a girl
Go limp
"It is a tactic"
I think.

"America!?" "Yes."
"But you are like
my aunt's cousin
who married so-and-so."
"Yes, (I say), I know."

On my knees
The earringed lady
Thinks I'm praying
She drops her sisal
and runs.

"You are a Negro?"
"Yes"
"But that is a kind of
food—isn't it—
the white man used to
eat you???"
"Well—"

Unusual things amuse us
A little African girl
Sees my white friend
And runs
She thinks he wants her
For his dinner.

The fresh corpse
Of a white rhinoceros
His horn gone
Some Indian woman
Will be approached
Tonight.

The man in the
Scarlet shirt
Wanted to talk
but had no words—
I had words
but no Scarlet
Shirt.

floating shakily down the
nile
on my rented raft
I try to be a native
queen
a prudent giraffe
on the bank
turns up
        his nose.

We eat Metoke*
with three fingers—
other things
get two fingers
and one of those
a thumb.

*A food staple of the Buganda in Uganda, made from plantains.

That you loved me
I felt sure
Twice you asked
me gently
if I liked the
strange
gray
stew.

Pinching both my legs
the old man kneels
before me on the
ground
his head white
Ah! Africa's mountain
peaks
Snow to grace
eternal spring!

To build a house
One needs mud
and sisal
And friendly
Neighbors.

Where the glacier was
A lake
Where the lake is
Sunshine
And redheaded
Marabou storks.

On a grumpy day
An African child
Chants "good morning"
—I have never seen
Such bright sun!

The Nairobi streets
At midnight
Deserted
The hot dog man
Folds up his cart.

In Nairobi
I pestered an
Indian boy to
Sell me a
Hat
For five shillings—
How bright
His eyes were!

In a kanzu
Long and white
Stands my African
Dad
The sound of drums
Fills
The air!

On my brother's motorcycle
The Indian mosques
And shops fade behind us
My hair takes flight
He laughs
He has not seen such hair
Before.

An African girl
Gives me a pineapple
Her country's national
Flower
How proudly she
Blinks the eye
Put out
By a sharp pineapple
Frond.
I wonder if I should
Kneel
At her bare little
Feet?

At first night
I sat alone
& watched the
        sun set
behind
        the
aberdares
        During
        the day
                my legs
and the sun
        belonged
        to
the village
        children.

Under the moon
luminous
huts. . . .
Brown breasts stuck
out to taunt
the sullen wind.

A crumbling
hut . . .
in the third
room
a red chenille
bedspread
(by Cannon)
a cracked
jar
of violet
        lilies
        (by?)

The native women
thought me
strange
until they
saw me follow you
to your house.

In Kampala
the young king
goes often
to Church
the young girls here
are
So pious.

Settled behind
tall banana trees
the little hut
is overcovered by
their leaves
patiently it waits
for autumn
which never comes. . . .

In my journal
I thought I could
capture
everything. . . .
Listen!
the soft wings of cranes
sifting the salt sea
air.

LOVE

A dark stranger
My heart searches
Him out
"Papa!"

An old man in white
Calls me "mama"
It does not take much
To know
He wants me for
His wife—
He has no teeth
But is kind.

The American from
Minnesota
Speaks Harvardly
of Revolution—
Men of the Mau Mau
Smile
Their fists
holding
Bits of
Kenya earth.

A tall Ethiopian
Grins at me
The grass burns
My bare feet.

Drums outside
My window
Morning whirls
In
I have danced all
Night.

The bearded Briton
Wears a shirt of
Kenya flags
I am at home
He says.

Down the hill
A grove of trees
And on this spot
The magic tree.

The Kenya air!
Miles of hills
Mountains
And holding both
My hands
A Mau Mau leader.

And in the hut
The only picture—
Of Jesus

Explain to the
Women
In the village
That you are
Twenty
And belong—
To no one.

KARAMOJONGS

A tall man
Without clothes
Beautiful
Like a statue
Up close
His eyes
Are running
Sores.

The Noble Savage
Erect
No shoes on his
feet
His pierced ears
Infected.

"Quite incredible—
your hair-do is
most divine——
Held together
With *cow* dung?
You mean——?!"
The lady stares
At her fingers.

A proper English meal
Near the mountains
"More tea, please."
Down the street
A man walks
Quite completely
Nude.

Bare breasts loose
In the sun
The skin cracked
The nipples covered
With flies
But she is an old
Woman
What?—twenty?

A Catholic church
The chaste cross
Stark
Against the purple sky.
We surprise a
couple there alone
In prayer?

There is no need for
Sadness
After the dying boy
There is the living girl
Who throws you a
kiss.

How bright the little
girl's
Eyes were!
a first sign of
Glaucoma.

The Karamojongs
Never civilized
A proud people
I think there
Are
A hundred left.

ONCE

i

Green lawn
a picket fence
flowers—
My friend smiles
she had heard
that Southern
jails
were drab.

Looking up I see
a strong arm
raised
the Law
Someone in America
is being
protected
       (from me.)

In the morning
there was
a man in gray
but the sky
was blue.

ii

"Look at that
nigger with those
white folks!"
       My dark
Arrogant friend
turns calmly, curiously
helpfully,
       "Where?" he
              asks.

It was the fifth
arrest
In as many
    days
How glad I am
that I can
look
surprised
              still.

iii

Running down
Atlanta
      streets
With my sign
I see heads
      turn
Eyes
     goggle
"a nice girl
  like her!"

A Negro cook
assures
      her mistress—

But I had seen
the fingers
near her eyes
   wet with
    tears.

iv

One day in
Georgia
Working around
the Negro section
My friend got a
letter
in
the mail
—the letter
said
    "I hope you're
having a good
time
fucking all
        the niggers."

"Sweet," I winced.
        "Who
              wrote it?"

"mother."
        she
              said.

That day she sat
        a long time
a little black girl
in pigtails
on her lap

Her eyes were very
Quiet.

She used to tell the big colored ladies
her light eyes just
the same
"I am alone
my mother died."
Though no other
letter
came.

v

It is true—
I've always loved
the daring
                ones
Like the black young
man
Who tried
to crash
All barriers
at once,
    wanted to
swim
At a white
beach (in Alabama)
Nude.

vi
Peter always
thought
the only
way to
"enlighten"
southern towns
was to
introduce
     himself
to
the county
sheriff
     first thing.

Another thing
Peter wanted—
was to be
cremated

but we
couldn't
find him
when he needed it.

But he was just a "yid"
seventeen.

vii

I
never liked
white folks
really
it
happened quite
suddenly
one
day
A pair of
amber
eyes
I
think
he
had.

viii
I *don't* think
integration
entered
into it
officer

You see
there was
this little
Negro
girl
Standing here
alone
and her
mother
went into
that store
there

then—
there came by

this little boy
  here
without his
  mother
& eating
  an
ice cream cone
—see there it is—
  strawberry

Anyhow

        and the little
         girl was
         hungry
          and
        stronger
          than
        the little
         boy—

Who is too
  fat
  really,
        anyway.

ix

Someone said
     to
        me
that
   if
      the South
rises
    again
it will do so
   "from
the grave."

Someone
      else
        said
if the South
  rises
     again
he would

"step
on
it."

Dick Gregory
said that
if the
South
rises
again
there is
a
secret
plan.

But I say—
if the
South
rises
again
It will not
do
so
in my presence.

x

"but I don'
really
          give a fuck
Who
     my daughter
          marries—"
the lady
was
adorable—
it was in a
tavern
i remember
her daughter
sat there
beside her
tugging
at
her arm
sixteen—

very shy
        and
very pim
        pled.

xi

then there
was
the charming
     half-wit
who told
the judge
re: indecent exposure
"but when I
step out
  of the
  tub
I look
  Good—
just because
my skin
is black
don't mean
it ain't
pretty
     you old bastard!)
what will we

finally do
with prejudice?

some people like
to take a walk
after a bath.

xii
"look, honey"
said
the
blond
amply
boobed
babe
in the
green
  g
string

"i like you
sure
i ain't
prejudiced

but the
lord didn't
give me
legs

like
these
because
he
wanted
to see'm
dangling
from a
poplar!"

"But they're so
        much
                prettier
                        than mine.

Would you really mind?"
he asked
wanting her to dance.

xiii
I remember
seeing
a little girl,
dreaming—perhaps,
  hit by
    a
  van truck

"That nigger was
in the way!" the
man
    said
      to
understanding cops.

    But was she?
    She was
      just eight
        her mother

said
and little
for
her age.

xiv

then there was
the
picture of
the
bleak-eyed
little black
girl
waving the
american
flag
holding it
gingerly
with
the very
tips
of her
fingers.

CHIC FREEDOM'S REFLECTION

(for Marilyn Pryce)

One day
Marilyn marched
beside me (demon-
stration)
and we ended up
at county farm
no phone
no bail
something about
"traffic vio-
lation"
which irrelevance
Marilyn dismissed
with a shrug
    She
had just got
    back
from
    Paris France
       In
     the

Alabama
hell
she
smell-
ed
so
wonderful
like spring
& love
&
freedom
She
wore a
SNCC pin*
right between
her breasts
near her
heart
& with a chic
(on "jail?")
accent
& nod of
condescent
to frumpy
work-house
hags

*The Student Non-Violent Coordinating Committee.

powdered her nose
       tip-
               toe
in a badge.

SOUTH:
THE NAME OF HOME

all that night
I prayed for eyes to see again
whose last sight
had been
a broken bottle
held negligently
in a racist
fist
God give us trees to plant
and hands and eyes to
love them.

When I am here again
the years of ease between
fall away
The smell of one
magnolia
sends my heart running
through the swamps.

the earth is red
here—
the trees bent, weeping
what secrets will not
the ravished land
reveal
of its abuse?

an old mistress
of my mother's
gives me
bloomers for christmas
ten sizes
too big
her intentions are
good my father
says
but typical—
neither the color
she knows
nor the
    number.

HYMN

I well remember
A time when
"Amazing Grace" was
All the rage
In the South.
"Happy" black mothers arguing
Agreement with
Illiterate sweating preachers
Hemming and hawing blessedness
Meekness
Inheritance of earth, e.g.,
Mississippi cotton fields?

And in the North
Roy Hamilton singing
"What is America to me?"
Such a good question
From a nice slum
In North Philly.

My God! the songs and
The people and the lives
Started here—
Weaned on "happy" tears
Black fingers clutching black teats
On black Baptist benches—
Some mother's troubles that everybody's
Seen
And nobody wants to see.

I can remember the rocking of
The church
And embarrassment
At my mother's shouts
Like it was all—"her happiness"—
Going to kill her.
My father's snores
Punctuating eulogies
His loud singing
Into fluffy gray caskets
A sleepy tear
In his eye.

Amazing Grace
How sweet the sound
That saved a wretch
Like me
I once was lost
But now I'm found
Was blind

But now
I see.

Mahalia Jackson, Clara Ward, Fats Waller,
Ray Charles,
Sitting here embarrassed with me
Watching the birth
Hearing the cries
Bearing witness
To the child,
Music.

THE DEMOCRATIC ORDER:
SUCH THINGS IN TWENTY
YEARS I UNDERSTOOD

My father
(back blistered)
beat me
because I
could not
stop crying.
He'd had
enough 'fuss'
he said
for one damn
voting day.

THEY WHO FEEL DEATH

(for martyrs)

They who feel death close as a breath
Speak loudly in unlighted rooms
Lounge upright in articulate gesture
Before the herd of jealous Gods

Fate finds them receiving
At home.

Grim the warrior forest who present
Casual silence with casual battle cries
Or stand unflinchingly lodged

In common sand
Crucified.

ON BEING ASKED TO LEAVE
A PLACE OF HONOR FOR ONE
OF COMFORT; PREFERABLY
IN THE NORTHERN SUBURBS

*(for those who work and stay in the
ragged Mississippis of the world)*

In this place of helmets and tar
the anxious burblings of recreants
buzz over us
we bent laughing to oars of gold

We regard them as Antigone her living kin

Fat chested pigeons
resplendent of prodigious riches
reaped in body weight
taking bewildered pecks
at eagles
as though *muck*
were God.

THE ENEMY

in gray, battle-scarred Leningrad
a tiny fist unsnapped to show
crumpled heads
of pink and yellow flowers
snatched hurriedly on the go
in the cold spring shower—

consent or not
countries choose
cold or hot
win or lose
to speak of wars
yellow and red
but there is much
let it be said
for children.

COMPULSORY
CHAPEL

A quiet afternoon
the speaker
dull
the New Testament
washed out
Through the window
a lonely
     blue-jay
makes noisy song.

The speaker crashes
on
through his speech
All eyes are
upon him
Over his left
ear
the thick hair
is beginning
to slip.

I would not mind
    if I were

              a sinner,

but as it is
—let me assure you—
I sleep alone.

To the Man
in the Yellow Terry

Dawn came at six today
Held back by hope
A lost cause—
Melted like snow
In the middle of
The day.

The sun shines clear fire
The earth once more
Like it was—
Old promises
Rise up
(Our honored
   Ghosts)
And the lonely truths
Of love
Pledged.

Here we lie
You and I—
Your mind, unaccountable,

My mind simply
Stopped—
Like a clock struck
By the treachery
Of time.

The sky blue, empty,
Unfathomable—
As I am.
Look at it brighten
And fill and
Astonish
With each movement
Of your
Eyes.

The wren who does not
Sing
I take my simple
Flight
Silent, unmetaphoric
Dressed in brown
I say
Good-bye.

Will you think it funny
Later on
To find you had

Almost
Given shelter
To a
Thief?

THE KISS

i was kissed once
by a beautiful man
all blond and
             czech
riding through bratislava
on a motor bike
screeching "don't yew let me fall off heah naow!"

the funny part was
he spoke english
and setting me gallantly
on my feet
kissed me for
not anyhow *looking*
like aunt jemima.

WHAT OVID
TAUGHT ME

What does it matter? you ask
If protocol
falls
After artichokes
and steak,
Vivaldi
and
No
Wine

For God's sake
Let's not be traditional!

But I,
Unused bed
All tousled
Sing nursery rhymes
Chant
Strange
Chants

Count stray insects
On the ceiling
and
Wonder—

Why don't you shut up and
get in?

MORNINGS / *of an impossible love*

On the morning you woke beside me—already thinking of going away—the sun did not fill my window as it does most mornings. Instead there was cloud and threat of snow. How I wish it could always be this way—that on mornings it cannot come itself, the sun might send me you.

Watching you frown at your face in the mirror this morning
I almost thought you disapproved of the little dark shadow
standing behind you its arms around your waist. . . .

Two mornings ago you left my little house. Only two steps from my fingers & you were gone, swallowed down swiftly by my spiral stairs. . . .

Why do you wish to give me over to someone else? "Such and such young man you're sure to like" you say "for he is a fine, cheerful fellow, very sensitive" and one thing and another. Sometimes it is as if you'd never listened to my heartbeat, never heard my breathing in your ear, never seen my eyes when you say such things. . . .

This is what you told me once. Must I believe you? "We are really Easterners, you and I. The rising of the Sun brings with it our whole Philosophy."

SO WE'VE COME
AT LAST
TO FREUD

Do not hold my few years
                          against me
In my life, childhood
                     was a myth
So long ago it seemed, even
                            in the cradle.

Don't label my love with slogans;
My father can't be blamed
                          for my affection
Or lack of it;
ask him.
He won't understand you.

Don't sit on holy stones
                        as you,
Loving me
         and hating me, condemn.
There is no need for that.

I like to think that I, though

                young it's true,

Know what

        I'm doing.

That I, once unhappy, am
Now
Quite sanely
        jubilant,
& that neither you
Nor I can
Deny
That no matter how
"Sick"
The basis
is
Of what we have,
What we *do* have
Is Good.

JOHANN

You look at me with children
In your eyes,
    Blond, blue-eyed
Teutons
Charmingly veiled
In bronze
    Got from me.

What would Hitler say?

I am brown-er
Than a jew
Being one step
Beyond that Colored scene.
You are the Golden Boy,
Shiny but bloody
And with that ancient martial tune
Only your heart is out of step—
You love.

But even knowing love
I shrink from you. Blond
And Black; it is too charged a combination.
Charged with past and present wars,
Charged with frenzy
and with blood

Dare I kiss your German mouth?
Touch the perfect muscles
Underneath the yellow shirt
Blending coolly
With your yellow
Hair?

I shudder at the whiteness
Of your hands.

Blue is too cold a color
for eyes.

But white, I think, is the color
Of honest flowers,

And blue is the color
Of the sky.

Come closer then and hold out to me
Your white and faintly bloodied hands.
I will kiss your German mouth
And will touch the helpless

White skin, gone red,
Beneath the yellow shirt.
I will rock the yellow head against
My breast, brown and yielding.

But I tell you, love,
There is still much to fear.
We have only seen the
First of wars
First of frenzies
First of blood.

Someday, perhaps, we will be
Made to learn
That blond and black
Cannot love.

But until that rushing day
I will not reject you.
I will kiss your fearful
German mouth.
And you—
Look at me boldly
With surging, brown-blond teutons
In your eyes.

THE SMELL
OF LEBANON

in balmy
      iconic
prague
I offered
my bosom
      to a wandering arab student
who spoke
much
of
Lebanon
    and
      his father's
        orchards

            it
          was near
          a castle
           near
          a river
           near
          the sun

```
                                   and
                                   warm
                  &
                  where he
                  bent
                  and kissed
                        me
                  on the swelling
                  brown
                  smelled for
                  a short
                        lingering
                              time
                  of
                     apples.
```

WARNING

To love a man wholly
love him
feet first
      head down
      eyes cold
      closed
in depression.

It is too easy to love
a surfer
white eyes
godliness &
          bronze
in the bright sun.

THE BLACK PRINCE

Very proud
he barely asked directions
to a nearby
hotel
    but no
    tired-eyed
    little village chief
    should spend his
    first night
    in chilly London
    alone.

MEDICINE

Grandma sleeps with
my sick
        grand-
pa so she
can get him
during the night
medicine
to stop
   the pain

In
the morning
clumsily
I
wake
them

Her eyes
look at me
from under-
        neath

his withered
arm

The
medicine
is all
in
her long
un-
braided
hair.

BALLAD OF
THE BROWN GIRL

I've got two
hundred
      dollars
the girl said
on her head
she wore a
school cap
—blue—
& brown she
looked no
more than
ten
but a freshman in
college?
well, hard
to tell—

I'll give you
'three hundred'
'fo' hunna'
'five wads of jack'

but "*mrs.* whatsyourname . . ."
the doctor says
with impatiently tolerant
eyes
you should *want*
it
you know . . .
talk it over with
your folks
you *may* be
                    surprised. . . .

the next morning
her slender
neck broken
her note short
and of cryptic
collegiate
make—

          just

"Question—

did ever brown
daughter to black
father a white
baby
        take—?"

SUICIDE

First, suicide notes should be
(not long) but written
second,
all suicide notes
should be signed
in blood
by hand
and to the point—
that point being, perhaps,
that there is none.
Thirdly, if it is the thought
of rest that
fascinates
laziness should be admitted
in the clearest terms.
Then, all things done
ask those outraged
consider their happiest
summer
& tell if the days it
adds up to
is one.

EXCUSE

Tonight it is the wine (or not the wine)
or a letter from you (or not a letter from you)
I sit
listen to the complacency of the rain
write a poem, kill myself there

It brings less pain—

Tonight it rains, tomorrow will be bright
tomorrow I'll say "yesterday was the same
only the rain . . .

and my shoes too tight."

TO DIE
BEFORE ONE WAKES
MUST BE GLAD

to die before one
wakes
must be glad

                            (to the same extent
                            maybe
                               that it is also
                            sad)

a slipping away
in glee
unobserved and
free
in the wide—

area felt spatially,
heart intact.

to die before one
wakes
must be joyous
full swing glorious
(rebellion)

(victory)
unremarked triumph

                                        love letters untorn
                                        foetal fears
                                        unborn
                                        monsters given
                                        berth

(love unseen, guiltily,
as creation)
                (life "good")

to die before one
wakes
must be a dance

                                        (perhaps a jig)
                                        and visual-

skipping tunes of
color
across smirking
eyelids
happy bluely . . .
though running gaily
out and out.

to die before one
wakes
must be
nice
(green little passions

red dying
into ice
spinningly
 (like a circus)

the blurred landscape
of the runner's
hurried
mile)
one's lips curving
sweetly
in one's most subtle smile.

EXERCISES ON THEMES FROM LIFE

i

Speaking of death
and decay
It hardly matters
Which
Since both are on the
way, maybe—
to being daffodils.

ii
It is not about that
a poet I knew used
to say
speaking with haunted eyes
of liking and disliking—
Now I think
uncannily
of life.

iii

My nausea has nothing
to do
With the fact that
you love me
It is probably just
something I ate
at your mother's.

iv

To keep up a
passionate courtship
with a tree
one must be
completely mad
In the forest
in the dark one night
I lost my way.

v

If I were a patriot
I would kiss the flag
As it is,
Let us just go.

vi

My father liked very much
the hymns
in church
in the amen corner,
on rainy days
he would wake
himself up
to hear them.

vii
I like to see you try
to worm yourself
away from me
first you plead
your age
as if my young heart
felt any of the tiredness
in your bones . . .

viii
Making our bodies touch
across your breezy bed
how warm you are . . .
cannot we save our little
quarrel
until tomorrow?

ix
My fear of burial
is all tied up with
how used I am
to the spring . . . !

Revolutionary
Petunias
& Other Poems

In 1966, I left my job with the New York City Welfare Department and returned South, to Mississippi, to work in the Voter Registration campaign. I fell almost immediately in love with a soulful young Jewish law student named Mel Leventhal who was also active in the campaign. The following year we were married, in New York, shortly before interracial marriage became legal in the South; we returned to live in Mississippi for the next seven years. Our daughter was born there.

It was a time of intense friendships, passions, and loves among the people who came South (or lived there), and who risked everything to change an oppressive, racist system; but as the years went by, there was a palpable increase among these same people of distrust, hatred, and intolerance.

These poems reflect my delight at being once again in a Southern African-American environment, and also my growing realization that the sincerest struggle to change the world must start within. I was saved from despair countless times by the flowers and the trees I planted.

These poems are about Revolutionaries and Lovers; and about the loss of compassion, trust, and the ability to expand in love that marks the end of hopeful strategy. Whether in love or revolution. They are also about (and for) those few embattled souls who remain painfully committed to beauty and to love even while facing the firing squad.

Humbly for George Jackson, who could "still smile sometimes. . . ." Whose eyes warmed to life until the end; whose face was determined, unconquered, and sweet.

And for my heroes, heroines, and friends of early SNCC, whose courage and beauty burned me forever.

And for the Mississippi Delta legend of Bob Moses.

And for Winson Hudson and Fannie Lou Hamer, whose strength and compassion I cherish.

And for my friend Charles Merrill, the artist, who paints skies.

And for Mel, the Trouper's father, who daily fights and daily loves, from a great heart.

IN THESE
DISSENTING TIMES

*To acknowledge our ancestors means
we are aware that we did not make
ourselves, that the line stretches
all the way back, perhaps, to God; or
to Gods. We remember them because it
is an easy thing to forget: that we
are not the first to suffer, rebel,
fight, love and die. The grace with
which we embrace life, in spite of
the pain, the sorrows, is always a
measure of what has gone before.*

In These Dissenting Times

I shall write of the old men I knew
And the young men
I loved
And of the gold toothed women
Mighty of arm
Who dragged us all
To church.

i

The Old Men Used to Sing

The old men used to sing
And lifted a brother
Carefully
Out the door
I used to think they
Were born
Knowing how to
Gently swing
A casket
They shuffled softly
Eyes dry
      More awkward
With the flowers
Than with the widow
After they'd put the
Body in
And stood around waiting
In their
Brown suits.

ii
Winking at a Funeral

Those were the days
Of winking at a
Funeral
Romance blossomed
In the pews
Love signaled
Through the
Hymns
What did we know?

Who smelled the flowers
Slowly fading?
Knew the arsonist
Of the church?

iii
Women

They were women then
My mama's generation
Husky of voice—Stout of
Step
With fists as well as
Hands
How they battered down
Doors
And ironed
Starched white
Shirts
How they led
Armies
Headragged Generals
Across mined
Fields
Booby-trapped
Kitchens
To discover books
Desks
A place for us

How they knew what we
Must know
Without knowing a page
Of it
Themselves.

iv
Three Dollars Cash

Three dollars cash
For a pair of catalog shoes
Was what the midwife charged
My mama
For bringing me.
"We wasn't so country then," says Mom,
"You being the last one—
And we couldn't, like
We done
When she brought your
Brother,
Send her out to the
Pen
And let her pick
Out
A pig."

You Had to Go
to Funerals

You had to go to funerals
Even if you didn't know the
People
Your Mama always did
Usually your Pa.
In new patent leather shoes
It wasn't so bad
And if it rained
The graves dropped open
And if the sun was shining
You could take some of the
Flowers home
In your pocket
book. At six and seven
The face in the gray box
Is always your daddy's
Old schoolmate
Mowed down before his
Time.
You don't even ask
After a while

What makes them lie so
Awfully straight
And still. If there's a picture of
Jesus underneath
The coffin lid
You might, during a boring sermon,
Without shouting or anything,
Wonder who painted it;

And how *he* would like
All eternity to stare
It down.

vi
Uncles

They had broken teeth
And billy club scars
But we didn't notice
Or mind
They were uncles.
It was their *job*
To come home every summer
From the North
And tell my father
He wasn't no man
And make my mother
Cry and long
For Denver, Jersey City,
Philadelphia.
They were uncles.
Who noticed how
Much
They drank
And acted womanish
With they do-rags
We were nieces.

And they were almost
Always good
For a nickel
Sometimes
a dime.

vii
They Take a Little Nip

They take a little nip
Now and then
Do the old folks

Now they've moved to
Town
You'll sometimes
See them sitting
Side by side
On the porch.

Straightly
As in church

Or working diligently
Their small
City stand of
Greens

Serenely pulling
Stalks and branches
Up
Leaving all
The weeds.

viii
Sunday School, Circa 1950

"Who made you?" was always
The question
The answer was always
"God."
Well, there we stood
Three feet high
Heads bowed
Leaning into
Bosoms.

Now
I no longer recall
The Catechism
Or brood on the Genesis
Of life
No.

I ponder the exchange
Itself
And salvage mostly
The leaning.

BURIAL

i

They have fenced in the dirt road
that once led to Wards Chapel
A.M.E. church,
and cows graze
among the stones that
mark my family's graves.
The massive oak is gone
from out the church yard,
but the giant space is left
unfilled;
despite the two-lane blacktop
that slides across
the old, unalterable
roots.

Today I bring my own child here;
to this place where my father's
grandmother rests undisturbed
beneath the Georgia sun,
above her the neatstepping hooves
of cattle.
Here the graves soon grow back into the land.
Have been known to sink. To drop open without
warning. To cover themselves with wild ivy,
blackberries. Bittersweet and sage.
No one knows why. No one asks.
When Burning Off Day comes, as it does
some years,
the graves are haphazardly cleared and snakes
hacked to death and burned sizzling
in the brush. . . . The odor of smoke, oak
leaves, honeysuckle.
Forgetful of geographic resolutions as birds,
the farflung young fly South to bury
the old dead.

The old women move quietly up
and touch Sis Rachel's face.
"Tell Jesus I'm coming," they say.
"Tell him I ain't goin' to *be*
long."

My grandfather turns his creaking head
away from the lavender box.
He does not cry. But looks afraid.
For years he called her "Woman";
shortened over the decades to
" 'Oman."
On the cut stone for " 'Oman's" grave
he did not notice
they had misspelled her name.
(The stone reads *Racher Walker*—not "Rachel"—
Loving Wife, Devoted Mother?)

iv

As a young woman, who had known her? Tripping
eagerly, "loving wife," to my grandfather's
bed. Not pretty, but serviceable. A hard
worker, with rough, moist hands. Her own two
babies dead before she came.
Came to seven children.
To aprons and sweat.
Came to quiltmaking.
Came to canning and vegetable gardens
big as fields.
Came to fields to plow.
Cotton to chop.
Potatoes to dig.
Came to multiple measles, chickenpox,
and croup.
Came to water from springs.
Came to leaning houses one story high.
Came to rivalries. Saturday night battles.
Came to straightened hair, Noxzema, and
feet washing at the Hardshell Baptist church.
Came to zinnias around the woodpile.

Came to grandchildren not of her blood
whom she taught to dip snuff without
sneezing.

Came to death blank, forgetful of it all.

When he called her " 'Oman" she no longer
listened. Or heard, or knew, or felt.

v

It is not until I see my first grade teacher
review her body that I cry.
Not for the dead, but for the gray in my
first grade teacher's hair. For memories
of before I was born, when teacher and
grandmother loved each other; and later
above the ducks made of soap and the orange-
legged chicks Miss Reynolds drew over
my own small hand
on paper with wide blue lines.

vi

Not for the dead, but for memories. None of them sad. But seen from the angle of her death.

FOR MY SISTER MOLLY
WHO IN THE FIFTIES

Once made a fairy rooster from
Mashed potatoes
Whose eyes I forget
But green onions were his tail
And his two legs were carrot sticks
A tomato slice his crown.
Who came home on vacation
When the sun was hot
and cooked
and cleaned
And minded least of all
The children's questions
A million or more
Pouring in on her
Who had been to school
And knew (and told us too) that certain
Words were no longer good
And taught me not to say us for we
No matter what "Sonny said" up the
road.

FOR MY SISTER MOLLY WHO IN THE FIFTIES

Knew Hamlet well and read into the night
And coached me in my songs of Africa
A continent I never knew
But learned to love
Because "they" she said could carry
A tune
And spoke in accents never heard
In Eatonton.
Who read from *Prose and Poetry*
And loved to read "Sam McGee from Tennessee"
On nights the fire was burning low
And Christmas wrapped in angel hair
And I for one prayed for snow.

WHO IN THE FIFTIES

Knew all the written things that made
Us laugh and stories by
The hour   Waking up the story buds
Like fruit. Who walked among the flowers
And brought them inside the house
And smelled as good as they
And looked as bright.
Who made dresses, braided
Hair. Moved chairs about
Hung things from walls
Ordered baths

Frowned on wasp bites
And seemed to know the endings
Of all the tales
I had forgot.

WHO OFF INTO THE UNIVERSITY

Went exploring   To London and
To Rotterdam
Prague and to Liberia
Bringing back the news to us
Who knew none of it
But followed
crops and weather
funerals and
Methodist Homecoming;
easter speeches,
groaning church.

WHO FOUND ANOTHER WORLD

Another life   With gentlefolk
Far less trusting
And moved and moved and changed
Her name
And sounded precise
When she spoke   And frowned away
Our sloppishness.

WHO SAW US SILENT

Cursed with fear   A love burning
Inexpressible
And sent me money not for me
But for "College."
Who saw me grow through letters
The words misspelled   But not
The longing   Stretching
Growth
The tied and twisting
Tongue
Feet no longer bare
Skin no longer burnt against
The cotton.

WHO BECAME SOMEONE OVERHEAD

A light   A thousand watts
Bright and also blinding
And saw my brothers cloddish
And me destined to be
Wayward
My mother remote   My father
A wearisome farmer
With heartbreaking
Nails.

FOR MY SISTER MOLLY WHO IN THE FIFTIES

Found much
Unbearable
Who walked where few had
Understood   And sensed our
Groping after light
And saw some extinguished
And no doubt mourned.

FOR MY SISTER MOLLY WHO IN THE FIFTIES

Left us.

EAGLE ROCK

In the town where I was born
There is a mound
Some eight feet high
That from the ground
Seems piled up stones
In Georgia
Insignificant.

But from above
The lookout tower
Floor
An eagle widespread
In solid gravel
Stone
Takes shape
Below;

The Cherokees raised it
Long ago
Before westward journeys
In the snow

Before the
National Policy slew
Long before Columbus knew.

I used to stop and
Linger there
Within the cleanswept tower stair
Rock Eagle pinesounds
Rush of stillness
Lifting up my hair.

Pinned to the earth
The eagle endures
The Cherokees are gone
The people come on tours.
And on surrounding National
Forest lakes the air rings
With cries
The silenced make.

Wearing cameras
They never hear
But relive their victory
Every year
And take it home
With them.
Young Future Farmers
As paleface warriors
Grub
Live off the land

Pretend Indian, therefore
Man,
Can envision a lake
But never a flood
On earth
So cleanly scrubbed
Of blood:
They come before the rock
Jolly conquerors.

They do not know the rock
They love
Lives and is bound
To bide its time
To wrap its stony wings
Around
The innocent eager 4-H Club.

BAPTISM

They dunked me in the creek;
a tiny brooklet.
Muddy, gooey with rotting leaves,
a greenish mold floating;
definable.
For love it was. For love of God
at seven. All in white.
With God's mud ruining my snowy
socks and his bullfrog spoors
gluing up my face.

J, My Good Friend
(ANOTHER FOOLISH INNOCENT)

It is too easy not to like
Jesus,
It worries greatness
To an early grave
Without any inkling
Of what is wise.

So when I am old,
And so foolish with pain
No one who knows
me
Can tell from which
Senility or fancy
I deign to speak,
I may sing
In my cracked and ugly voice
Of Jesus my good
Friend;
Just as the old women
In my home town
Do now.

VIEW FROM ROSEHILL CEMETERY: VICKSBURG

for Aaron Henry

Here we have watched ten thousand
seasons
come and go.
And unmarked graves atangled
in the brush
turn our own legs to trees
vertical forever between earth
and sun.
Here we are not quick to disavow
the pull of field and wood
and stream;
we are not quick to turn
upon our dreams.

Beauty, no doubt, does not make revolutions. But a day will come when revolutions will have need of beauty.

—ALBERT CAMUS, *The Rebel*

REVOLUTIONARY PETUNIAS

for June and Julius

REVOLUTIONARY PETUNIAS

Sammy Lou of Rue
sent to his reward
the exact creature who
murdered her husband,
using a cultivator's hoe
with verve and skill;
and laughed fit to kill
in disbelief
at the angry, militant
pictures of herself
the Sonneteers quickly drew:
not any of them people that
she knew.
A backwoods woman
her house was papered with
funeral home calendars and
faces appropriate for a Mississippi
Sunday School. She raised a George,
a Martha, a Jackie and a Kennedy. Also
a John Wesley Junior.
"Always respect the word of God,"

she said on her way to she didn't
know where, except it would be by
electric chair, and she continued
"Don't yall forgit to *water*
my purple petunias."

EXPECT NOTHING

Expect nothing. Live frugally
On surprise.
Become a stranger
To need of pity
Or, if compassion be freely
Given out
Take only enough
Stop short of urge to plead
Then purge away the need.

Wish for nothing larger
Than your own small heart
Or greater than a star;
Tame wild disappointment
With caress unmoved and cold
Make of it a parka
For your soul.

Discover the reason why
So tiny human giant

Exists at all
So scared unwise
But expect nothing. Live frugally
On surprise.

BE NOBODY'S DARLING

for Julius Lester

Be nobody's darling;
Be an outcast.
Take the contradictions
Of your life
And wrap around
You like a shawl,
To parry stones
To keep you warm.

Watch the people succumb
To madness
With ample cheer;
Let them look askance at you
And you askance reply.

Be an outcast;
Be pleased to walk alone
(Uncool)
Or line the crowded
River beds

With other impetuous
Fools.

Make a merry gathering
On the bank
Where thousands perished
For brave hurt words
They said.

Be nobody's darling;
Be an outcast.
Qualified to live
Among your dead.

REASSURANCE

I must love the questions
themselves
as Rilke said
like locked rooms
full of treasure
to which my blind
and groping key
does not yet fit.

and await the answers
as unsealed
letters
mailed with dubious intent
and written in a very foreign
tongue.

and in the hourly making
of myself
no thought of Time
to force, to squeeze
the space
I grow into.

Nothing Is Right

Nothing is right
that does not work.
We have believed it all:
improvement, progress,
bigger, better, immediate,
fast.
The whole Junk.

It was our essence that
never worked.
We hasten to eradicate
our selves.

Consider the years
of rage and wrench and
mug.
What was it kept
the eyes alive?
Declined to outmode
the
hug?

CRUCIFIXIONS

I am not an idealist, nor a cynic,
but merely unafraid of contradictions.
I have seen men face each other when
both were right, yet each was determined
to kill the other, which was wrong.
What each man saw was an image of the
other, made by someone else. That is
what we are prisoners of.
  —A PERSONAL TESTAMENT BY DONALD HOGAN,
    Harper's Magazine, January 1972

BLACK MAIL

Stick the finger inside
the chink;
nail long and sharp.
Wriggle it,
jugg,
until it draws blood.
Lick it in your mouth,
savor the taste;
and know your diet
has changed.

Be the first at the crucifixion.
Stand me (and them and her and him)
where once we each together
stood.
Find it plausible now
to jeer,
escaped within your armor.
There never was a crucifixion
of a completely armored man.

Imagine this: a suit of mail,
of metal plate;
no place to press the dagger in.
Nothing but the eyes
to stick
with narrow truth.
Burning sharp,
burning bright;
burning righteous,
but burning blind.

LONELY PARTICULAR

When the people knew you
That other time
You were not as now
A crowding General,
Firing into your own
Ranks;
Forcing the tender skin
Of men
Against the guns
The very sun
To mangled perfection
For your cause.

Not General then
But frightened boy.
The cheering fell
Within the quiet
That fed your
Walks

Across the mines.
A mere foot soldier,
Marching the other way;
A lonely Particular.

.

PERFECTION

Having reached perfection
as you have
there no longer exists
the need for love.
Love is ablution
the dirtied is due
the sinner can
use.

THE GIRL WHO DIED #1

"Look!" she cried.
"I am not perfect
but still your sister.
Love me!"
But the mob beat her and kicked her
and shaved her head;
until she saw exactly
how wrong she was.

ENDING

I so admired you then;
before the bloody ending
of the story
cured your life
of all belief.
I would have wished
you alive
still. Or even
killed.
Before this thing we
got,
with flailing arms
and venomous face
took our love away.

LOST MY VOICE? OF COURSE.

*for Beanie**

Lost my voice?
Of course.

You said "Poems of
love and flowers are
a luxury the Revolution
cannot afford."

Here are the warm and juicy
vocal cords,
slithery,
from my throat.

Allow me to press them upon
your fingers,
as you have pressed
that bloody voice of yours
in places it could not know
to speak,
nor how to trust.

*A childhood bully.

The Girl Who Died #2

for d.p.

No doubt she was a singer
of naughty verse
and hated judgments
(black and otherwise)
and wove a life
of stunning contradiction,
was driven mad
by obvious
professions
and the word
"sister"
hissed by snakes
belly-low,
poisonous,
in the grass.
Waiting with sex
or tongue
to strike.

Behold the brothers!

They strut behind
the casket
wan and sad
and murderous.
Thinking whom
to blame
for making this girl
die
alone, lashed
denied
into her room.

This girl who would not lie;
and was not born
to be "correct."

THE OLD WARRIOR TERROR

Did you hear?
After everything
the Old Warrior Terror
died a natural death at home,
in bed.
Just reward
for having proclaimed abroad
that True Believers never
doubt;
True Revolutionaries never
smile.

Judge Every One with Perfect Calm

Follow the train full of bodies;
listening in the tiny wails
for reassurance of your mighty
right. Ride up and down the gorges
on your horse
collecting scalps.
Your creed is simple, and even
true: We learn from each other
by doing. Period.

Judge every one with perfect calm.
Stand this man here and that one
there;
mouths begging open holes.
Let them curtsey into the ditch
dug before them.
They will not recall tomorrow
your judgment of today.

THE QPP

The quietly pacifist peaceful
always die
to make room for men
who shout. Who tell lies to
children, and crush the corners
off of old men's dreams.
And now I find your name,
scrawled large in someone's
blood, on this survival
list.

HE SAID COME

He said come
Let me exploit you;
Somebody must do it
And wouldn't you
Prefer a brother?
Come, show me your
Face,
All scarred with tears;
Unburden your heart—
Before the opportunity
Passes away.

. . . *Or maybe the purpose of being
here, wherever we are, is to increase
the durability and the occasions of
love among and between peoples. Love,
as the concentration of tender caring
and tender excitement, or love as the
reasons for joy.* **I** *believe that love
is the single, true prosperity of any
moment and that whatever and whoever
impedes, diminishes, ridicules, opposes
the development of loving spirit is
"wrong"/hateful.*

—June Jordan

MYSTERIES

The man who slowly walked away from
them was a king in their society. A day
had come when he had decided that he
did not need any kingship other than the
kind of wife everybody would loathe
from the bottom of their hearts. He had
planned for that loathing in secret;
they had absorbed the shock in secret.
When everything was exposed, they had
only one alternative: to keep their preju-
dice and pretend Maru had died.

—Bessie Head, *Maru*

MYSTERIES

Your eyes are widely open flowers.
Only their centers are darkly clenched
To conceal Mysteries
That lure me to a keener blooming
Than I know,
And promise a secret
I must have.

i

the gift he gave unknowing
she already had
though feebly
lost
a planted thing
within herself
scarcely green
nearly severed

till he came

a magic root
sleeping beneath
branches
long grown wild.

ii

and when she thought of him
seated in the dentist's chair
she thought she understood
the hole she
discovered through
her tongue
as mysteries in
separate boxes
the space between them
charged
waiting till the feeling
should return.

iii
but she was known to be
unwise
and lovesick lover of motionless
things
wood and bits of clever
stone
a tree she cared for swayed overhead
in swoon
but would not follow
her.

iv
and his fingers peeled
the coolness off
her mind
his flower eyes crushed her
till
she bled.

GIFT

You intend no doubt
to give me nothing,
and are not aware
the gift has already been
received.
Curse me then,
and take away
the spell.
For I am rich;
no cheap and ragged
beggar
but a queen,
to rouse the king
I need in you.

CLUTTER-UP PEOPLE

The odd stillness of your body
excites a madness
in me.
I burn to know what it is like
awake.
Arching, rolling
across
my sky.
Your quiet litheness
as you move across the room is
a drug
that pulls me
under;
your leaving slays me.
Clutter-up people
casually track
the immaculate
corridor/passion
of my death

and blacken the empty air
with talk of war,
and other too comprehensible
things.

THIEF

I wish to own only the warmth
of your skin
the sound your thoughts make
reverberating off the coldness
of my loss
to love you purely
as I love trees and
the quiet sheens and
colors
of my house
my heart is full
of charity
of fair play
although on other
occasions
it has been acknowledged
I am a thief.

WILL

It does not impress me that I have
a mind.
Chance amuses me.
Coincidence makes me laugh
out loud.
Fate weighs me down
too heavy.

When I can't bear not seeing
you another second,
I send out my
will;
when it brings us face to
face,
there's an invisible power
I respect!

RAGE

In me there is a rage to defy
the order of the stars
despite their pretty patterns.
To see if Gods who hold forth now
on human thrones
can will away my lust
to dare
and press to order the anarchy
I would serve.

The silence between your words
rams into me
like a sword.

STORM

Throughout the storm and party
you chose to act the child
a two-year-old as distant as
the moon.
But our thunder and lightning God
obscured the age,
revealed the play,
and distinctly your age-old glance
shook the room.

WHAT THE FINGER WRITES

Your name scrawled on a bit of paper moves me.
And I should beware.
Take my dreaming self beyond the reach
of your cheery letters,
written laboriously with
stubby pencils and grubby
nails.

: What the finger writes the soul can read :

All life was spirit once
a disembodied groping across
the void;
toward the unknown otherness
the flesh is weak and slow
with luck I shall not live there
anymore.

FORBIDDEN THINGS

They say you are not for me,
and I try, in my resolved but
barely turning brain,
to know "they" do not matter,
these relics of past disasters
in march against the rebellion
of our time.

They will fail;
as all the others have:
for our fate *will not* be this:
to smile and salute the pain,
to limp behind their steel boot
of happiness,
grieving for forbidden things.

No Fixed Place

Go where you will.
Take the long lashes
that guard your eyes
and sweep a path
across this earth;
but see if it is not true
that voluptuous blood,
though held to the tinkling
quiet of a choked back
stream,
will yet rush out
to aid shy love,
and flood out the brain
to make a clean
and sacred place
for itself;
though there is no fixed place
on earth for man
or woman.
It will not help
that you believe
in miracles.

NEW FACE

I have learned not to worry about love;
but to honor its coming
with all my heart.
To examine the dark mysteries
of the blood
with headless heed and
swirl,
to know the rush of feelings
swift and flowing
as water.
The source appears to be
some inexhaustible
spring
within our twin and triple
selves;
the new face I turn up
to you
no one else on earth
has ever
seen.

THE NATURE OF THIS FLOWER
IS TO BLOOM

*And for ourselves, the intrinsic
"Purpose" is to reach, and to remember,
and to declare our commitment to all
the living, without deceit, and without
fear, and without reservation. We do
what we can. And by doing it, we keep
ourselves trusting, which is to say,
vulnerable, and more than that,
what can anyone ask?*
—JUNE JORDAN, IN A PERSONAL LETTER, 1970

While Love Is Unfashionable

for Mel

While love is unfashionable
let us live
unfashionably.
Seeing the world
a complex ball
in small hands;
love our blackest garment.
Let us be poor
in all but truth, and courage
handed down
by the old
spirits.
Let us be intimate with
ancestral ghosts
and music
of the undead.

While love is dangerous
let us walk bareheaded
beside the Great River.
Let us gather blossoms
under fire.

BEYOND WHAT

We reach for destinies beyond
what we have come to know
and in the romantic hush
of promises
perceive each
the other's life
as known mystery.
Shared. But inviolate.
No melting. No squeezing
into One.
We swing our eyes around
as well as side to side
to see the world.

To choose, renounce,
this, or that—
call it a council between equals
call it love.

The Nature of This Flower Is
to Bloom

Rebellious. Living.
Against the Elemental Crush.
A Song of Color
Blooming
For Deserving Eyes.
Blooming Gloriously
For its Self.

Revolutionary Petunia.

Good Night, Willie Lee, I'll See You in the Morning

I was shattered by the assassination of so many people I loved during the sixties. And by the resulting ugliness of spirit in many of those who had been most beautiful. In the early seventies my father died. By 1975 my marriage had ended. It was a time of barely holding on, as I felt myself changing, and not always knowing how or why. These are the poems of breakdown and spiritual disarray that led me eventually into a larger understanding of the psyche, and of the world. My years-long period of lamentation was finally ended when I realized I was capable not only of change, but of forgiveness, and could assume that others were also. For it is change in the self, along with the ability to forgive the self and others, that frees us for the next encounter.

Many years ago, a young romantic girl who had always modestly refrained from admitting her most secret belief (that her own people possessed the lion's share of beauty and goodness in the world) perceived the end was coming for them as they were and set out for The Last Land. There she wished to collect the saltysweet drops of sweat—the price of her people's goodness and beauty—from their rapidly freezing faces.

Wishing at least to observe what could not be prevented, she expected to see the end of sweaty beauty, and she did.

Everywhere she went she found that earlier visitors not so reverent as she (for with bullets and hatred they had come) had iced flat the warm, round faces she would have loved. Perhaps, here and there, a face had escaped and it would hold her rapt. She would quickly press it inside a large notebook she carried and her tears were payment for the theft.

But these were the faces of the old, those who would soon be dead.

She became quite discouraged.

But then she began to hear about a man no one could describe without first saying: "Well, he was a quiet man . . ." and her flagging heart revived and she began to look for him.

In the fields, underneath the trees, in small country stores, in the shabby new schools that housed the people's children.

Under the very noses of those who iced people daily, she looked.

But she did not find him.

The people said, "The quiet man always said, 'Let the people decide.'" And, though it did not seem quite the revolutionary thing to some of them, if the people wanted—in a particular village—to operate sewing machines, he would sit and sew with them. If they wanted to cook ribs, he would wash the pots. If they wanted to march, he was on the line.

If someone asked him anything (because they thought he was wise even though he had been to the white man's best schools) he would only reply, "Let the people decide."

"Oh, he was a quiet man," they told the romantic young girl, "and he loved women not just to lie with but he would stand up with them when no one else would. A quiet young man. A woman could speak in his company. A man could touch his shoulder with his hand and call out his own heart for review."

It so happened that the romantic young girl's own heart hungered for just this last experience.

But she never found him.

Even before she began her search he had disappeared from that land. He changed his name, they said; took his mother's name. Returned to his mother's far country, which was Africa.

The young romantic girl never saw his face, never heard his voice, never felt him stand up beside her, though it reassured her that he must be somewhere.

He became a memory of someone she had never known, a high standard.

And perhaps no one had known him. Perhaps he did not exist. Perhaps the people made up the quiet man because they needed him to exist. Perhaps if he did exist he was a fraud. So many people are.

But she chooses not to believe anything except that he does exist, and she dedicates this book to him, wherever in the world he is.

. . . and to my brothers: Fred, William, James, Robert, and Curtis

(and my friend Gloria)

. . . and in memory of our father's shining eyes.

CONFESSION

DID THIS HAPPEN TO YOUR MOTHER? DID YOUR SISTER THROW UP A LOT?

I love a man who is not worth
my love.
Did this happen to your mother?
Did your grandmother wake up
for no good reason
in the middle of the night?

I thought love could be controlled.
It cannot.
Only behavior can be controlled.
By biting your tongue purple
rather than speak.
Mauling your lips.
Obliterating his number
too thoroughly
to be able to phone.

Love has made me sick.

Did your sister throw up a lot?
Did your cousin complain

of a painful knot
in her back?
Did your aunt always
seem to have something else
troubling her mind?

I thought love would adapt itself
to my needs.
But needs grow too fast;
they come up like weeds.
Through cracks in the conversation.
Through silences in the dark.
Through everything you thought was concrete.

Such needful love has to be chopped out
or forced to wilt back,
poisoned by disapproval
from its own soil.

This is bad news, for the conservationist.

My hand shakes before this killing.
My stomach sits jumpy in my chest.
My chest is the Grand Canyon
sprawled empty
over the world.

Whoever he is, he is not worth all this.
Don't you agree?

And I will never
unclench my teeth long enough
to tell him so.

More Love to His Life

Though I at the time, had no one
and furthermore was dutifully told
how much he loved his wife,
he feared, he said,
I would reject him.
And so, the burden of adding more love
to his life
fell on me.

How could I refuse?
He needed the love of everyone.
I needed to understand this
though it did violence,
as they say,
to my heart.
Having no rights. No claims
to make, I could not even coherently
protest.

My heart, however, sent out darts
and messages

like red flags:
You are sending me away!
Stop! You are hurting me!
I love you more than anything
in my life!

But I laughed, over the phone,
as it occurred to me
that perhaps *he* was comic
instead of myself.

GIFT

He said: Here is my soul.
I did not want his soul
but I am a Southerner
and very polite.
I took it lightly
as it was offered. But did not
chain it down.
I loved it and tended
it. I would hand it back
as good as new.

He said: How dare you want
my soul! Give it back!
How greedy you are!
It is a trait
I had not noticed
before!

I said: But your soul
never left you. It was only
a heavy thought from

your childhood
passed to me for safekeeping.

But he never believed me.
Until the end
he called me possessive
and held his soul
so tightly
it shrank
to fit his hand.

Never Offer Your Heart
to Someone Who
Eats Hearts

Never offer your heart
to someone who eats hearts
who finds heartmeat
delicious
but not rare
who sucks the juices
drop by drop
and bloody-chinned
grins
like a God.

Never offer your heart
to a heart gravy lover.
Your stewed, overseasoned
heart consumed
he will sop up your grief
with bread
and send it shuttling
from side to side
in his mouth
like bubblegum.

If you find yourself
in love
with a person
who eats hearts
these things
you must do:

Freeze your heart
immediately.
Let him—next time
he examines your chest—
find your heart cold
flinty and unappetizing.

Refrain from kissing
lest he in revenge
dampen the spark
in your soul.

Now,
sail away to Africa
where holy women
await you
on the shore—
long having practiced the art
of replacing hearts
with God
and Song.

THREATENED

Threatened by my rising need
he writes
he is afraid
he may fail me
in performance.
But—I tell him—
I have failed
all my life—
only with you
do I nearly succeed.
My heart—which I feel
freezing a bit each day
to this man—nonetheless
cries: Don't leave her!
Don't go! She is counting
on you!
When we talk about it
nothing to still my fear

of his fear
is said

it is this fear
that now devours
desire.

MY HUSBAND SAYS

My husband says
this shortness of breath
and feeling of falling down a well
I suffer
in the half-life I share
with my lover
will soon cease to plague me.
That love, like war,
escalates
each side raising its demands
for what it wants
as emotions rise
higher and higher
and what was unthought of in the beginning
becomes the inevitable result.

"Soon you will write
you can not live without him
no matter that he has a wife.
He will tell you
the 1,000 miles separating you

is crushing to his soul.
As for me,
I love no one now
except you.
But if I am ever asked
in your presence
if this is true,
please don't take offense
at the vehemence
of my negative
reply."

CONFESSION

All winter long
I've borne the knife that presses
without ceasing
against my heart.
Despising lies
I have told everyone
the truth:
Truth is killing me.

THE INSTANT OF OUR PARTING

I said: I cannot tell you
how much I do not believe
in you
the instant we part.

I said: I lived in limbo
that whole summer
wondering if your love for me
would survive your flight
home.

I said: I am better now
that the instant we part
the instant of our parting
is with me always.

HE SAID:

He said: I want you to be happy.
He said: I love you so.
Then he was gone.
For two days I was happy.
For two days, he loved me so.
After that, I was on my own.

THE LAST TIME

The last time
I was afflicted by love
I murdered the man.
But that was in an earlier century
another country
a hotter climate
and death proved him
a foreign transient
like any other.

AFTER THE SHRINK

Without my melancholia I am lonely
dazed.
Under the doctor's care
I can remember nothing very long
that is sad.
Round and round I travel
enduring my comfort.

AT FIRST

At first I did not fight it.
I *loved* the suffering.
It was being alive!
I felt my heart pump the blood
that splashed my insides
with red flowers;
I savored my grief
like chilled wine.

I did not know my life
was being shredded
by an expert.

It was my friend Gloria
who saved me. Whose glance said "Really,
you've got to be kidding. Other
women have already done this
sort of suffering for you,
or so I thought."

ON
STRIPPING BARK
FROM MYSELF . . .

JANIE CRAWFORD

i love the way Janie Crawford

left her husbands   the one who wanted
to change her into a mule
and the other who tried to interest her
in being a queen
a woman unless she submits is neither a mule
nor a queen
though like a mule she may suffer
and like a queen pace
the floor

Moody

I am a moody woman
my temper as black as my brows
as sharp as my nails
as impartial as a flood
that is seeking, seeking, seeking
always
somewhere to stop.

NOW THAT THE BOOK IS FINISHED

Now that the book is finished,
now that I know my characters
will live,
I can love my child again.
She need sit no longer
at the back of my mind,
the lonely sucking of her thumb
a giant stopper in my throat.

HAVING EATEN TWO PILLOWS

*(for Bessie Head)**

Having eaten two pillows
in the middle of the night
having stumbled from bullets
my close friends have fired
having loved all those fully
that I love
and still not loving
all those to whom time
has not brought grace
ambition raises itself:
to survive my life
"just anyone"
        hello
though I know quite well
the words to say goodbye.

---

*In some of the fiction of South African writer Bessie Head, the ambition
of her characters is not to be extraordinary or considered extraordinary but
to become "just anyone," which is perceived as the correct relationship to
other people and to the world.
  I feel this is also a correct alternative to despair, or, in some cases, suicide.

LIGHT BAGGAGE

(for Zora,
*Nella, Jean)**

there is a magic
lingering after people
to whom success is merely personal.
who, when the public prepares a feast
for their belated acceptance parties,
pack it up like light baggage
and disappear into the swamps of Florida
or go looking for newer Gods
in the Oak tree country
of Pennsylvania.
or decide, quite suddenly, to try nursing,
midwifery, anonymous among the sick and the poor.
stories about such people
tell us little;
and if a hundred photographs survive

---

*Zora Neale Hurston, Nella Larson, and Jean Toomer wrote and published
their best work during the twenties and thirties. At some point in their
careers each of them left the "career" of writing and went off seeking writing's
very heart: life itself. Zora went back to her native Florida where she lived
in a one-room cabin and raised her own food; Jean Toomer became a
Quaker and country philosopher in Bucks County, Pennsylvania; and Nella
Larson, less well known than either Hurston or Toomer, became a nurse.

each one will show a different face.
someone out of step. alone out there, absorbed;
fishing in the waters of experience
a slouched back against the shoulders
of the world.

ON STRIPPING BARK
FROM MYSELF

(for Jane, who said trees die from it)

Because women are expected to keep silent about
their close escapes I will not keep silent
and if I am destroyed (naked tree!) someone will
   please
mark the spot
where I fall and know I could not live
silent in my own lies
hearing their "how *nice* she is!"
whose adoration of the retouched image
I so despise.

No. I am finished with living
for what my mother believes
for what my brother and father defend
for what my lover elevates
for what my sister, blushing, denies or rushes
to embrace.

I find my own
small person
a standing self

against the world
an equality of wills
I finally understand.

Besides:

My struggle was always against
an inner darkness: I carry within myself
the only known keys
to my death—to unlock life, or close it shut
forever. A woman who loves wood grains, the color
    yellow.
and the sun, I am happy to fight
all outside murderers
as I see I must.

EARLY LOSSES:
A REQUIEM

EARLY LOSSES: A REQUIEM

part i

Nyanu was appointed
as my Lord. The husband chosen
by the elders
before my birth.
He sipped wine with
my father
and when I was born
brought a parrot as
his gift
to play with me.
Paid baskets of grain
and sweet berries
to make me fat
for his pleasure.

Omunu was my playmate
who helped consume
Nyanu's gifts.
Our fat selves grew
together

knee and knee.
It was Omunu I wished
to share my tiny
playing house.

Him I loved as the sun
must seek and chase
its own reflection
across the sky.
My brothers, before you
turn away—

The day the savages came
to ambush our village
it was Nyanu who struggled
bravely
Omunu ran and hid
behind his parents' house.
He was a coward but
only nine
as was I; who trembled
beside him as we two
were stolen away
Nyanu's dead body
begging remembrance
of his tiny morsel
taken from his mouth.
Nor was I joyful that he was dead
only glad that now I would not have
to marry him.

Omunu clasped my hands
within the barkcloth pouch
and I his head
a battered flower
bent low
upon its stalk
Our cries pounded back
into our throats
by thudding blows
we could not see
our mothers' cries
at such a distance
we could not hear
and over the miles
we feasted on homesickness
our mothers' tears and
the dew
all we consumed of homeland
before we left.

At the great water Omunu fought
to stay with me
at such a tender age
our hearts we set
upon each other
as the retreating wave
brings its closest friend
upon its back.
We cried out in words
that met an echo

and Omunu vanished
down a hole that
smelled of blood and
excrement and death
and I was "saved"
for sport among
the sailors of the crew.
Only nine, upon a ship. My mouth
my body a mystery
that opened with each tearing
lunge. Crying for Omunu
who was not seen
again
by these eyes.

Listen to your sister, singing
in the field.
My body forced to receive
grain and wild berries
and milk so I could seem
a likely wench
—my mother's child
sold for a price. My father's
child again for sale.
I prayed to all our Gods
"Come down to me"
Hoist the burden no child
was meant to bear
and decipher the prayer
from within each song

—the song despised—
my belly become a stronghold
for a stranger
who will not recall
when he is two
the contours of
his mother's face.
See the savages turn back
my lips
and with hot irons
brand me neck and thigh.

I could not see the horizon
for the sky
a burning eye
the sun, beloved in the shade,
became an enemy
a pestle pounding long
upon my head.
You walked with me.
And when day sagged into night
some one of you of my own
choice
shared my rest. Omunu
risen from the ocean
out of the stomachs of whales
the teeth of sharks
lying beside me sleeping
knee and knee.
We could not speak always

of hearts
for in the morning if they
sold you
how could I flatten
a wrinkled face?
The stupor of dread
made smooth the look
that to my tormentors
was born erased.
I mourned for you. And if you died
took out my heart upon my lap
and rested it.

See me old at thirty
my sack of cotton weighted
to the ground. My hair
enough to cover a marble
my teeth like rattles
made of chalk
my breath a whisper
of decay.
The slack of my belly
falling to my knees.
I shrink to become a tiny size
a delicate morsel
upon my mother's knee
prepared like bread. The shimmering
of the sun a noise
upon my head.

To the child that's left
I offer a sound
without a promise
a clue
of what it means.

The sound itself is all.

PART II

The Child

A sound like a small wind
finding the door of a
hollow reed
my mother's farewell
glocked up from the back
of her throat

the sound itself is all

all I have
to remember a mother
I scarcely knew.
"Omunu" to me; who never knew
what "Omunu" meant. Whether home
or man or trusted God. "Omunu."
Her only treasure,
and never spent.

IN UGANDA AN EARLY KING

In Uganda an early king chose
his wives
from among the straight and lithe
who natural as birds of paradise
and the wild poinsettias
grow

(Did you ever see Uganda women? Dainty
are their fingers
genteel their footsteps on the sand)
and he brought them behind
the palace to a place constructed
like a farmer's fattening pen
with slats raised off the ground
and nothing for
an escapable door
he force-fed them bran and milk
until the milk ran down their
chins
off the bulging mounds that filled
their skins

their eyes quite disappeared
they grew too fat to stand
but slithered to the hole
that poured their dinner
enormous seals

Because? *He liked fat wives*
they showed him prosperous!
and if they up and burst
or tore their straining skins
across the splintered floor,
why, like balloons,
he bought some more.

FORGIVE ME IF MY PRAISES

i

Forgive me if my praises
do not come easily
I do not praise myself
I am the cause of (he says)
my father's failure.
Protecting me
turned him into
a coward.
I, who curbed his temper
and shaped his life.
Me, who now can not praise
my work.

ii

They said:
My father was not
a great man.
My father was a peasant
a serf.
The grandson of a slave.
My father was not a man.
They said.

iii

Even so—
Let me surprise you
with my love
turned to fear
that I would gladly
pretend away.

iv

Open your arms.
Take me on your lap.
Sing me a blues.
Be B.B. King to my
Mean Woman.

v

What I need I know
is a good satisfying love
with even one such as you
with open seed-sowing hands
on long arms
embracing me
with lips purple as
Tea Cake's

kisses warm

a shoulder firm
as the smooth
strong flanks of trees
to fight with me against
my evil dreams.

The Abduction of Saints

As it was with Christ, so it is with Malcolm
and with King.
Who could withstand the seldom flashing smile,
the call to dance among the swords and barbs
that were their words? The men leaning from
out the robes of saints,
good and wholly kind? Though come
at last to both fists clenched and Voice
to flatten the ears
of all the world.

You mock them who divide and keep score of what
each man gave. They gave us rebellion as pure love:
a beginning of the new man.

Christ too was man rebelling. Walking dusty roads,
    sweating
under the armpits. Loving the cool of evening beside
the ocean,
the people's greetings and barbecued chicken; cursing
    under

his breath
the bruise from his sandal and his donkey's diarrhea.
Don't let them fool you. He was himself a beginning
of the new man. His love in front.
His love and his necessary fist, behind. (Life,
ended at a point, always falls backward into the
little that was known of it.)

But see how this saint too is hung defenselessly
on walls, his strong hands pinned:
his pious look causes us to blush, for him.
He belongs to Caesar.

It is because his people stopped to tally and to count:
Perhaps he loved young men too much? Did he wear
    his hair
a bit too long, or short? Weren't the strategies
he proposed all wrong,
since of course they did not work?

It is because his people argued over him. Denounced
each other
in his name. When next they looked they hardly
    noticed
he no longer looked himself.

Who could imagine that timid form with Voice like
thunder
to make threats, a fist enlarged from decking
    merchants?

That milkwhite check, the bluebell eye, the cracked
heart of plaster
designed
for speedy decay.

Aha! said a cricket in the grass (ancient observer of
distracted cross examiners);

Now you've seen it, now you don't!

And the body
was stolen away.

MALCOLM

Those who say they knew you
offer as proof
an image stunted
by perfection.
Alert for signs of the man
to claim, one must believe
they did not know you at all
nor can remember the small, less popular
ironies of the Saint:
that you learned to prefer
all women free
and enjoyed a joke
and loved to laugh.

FACING THE WAY

(IN ANSWER TO YOUR SILLY QUESTION)

(for algernon)

people have eaten fried fish
with the people
sewn on sewing machines
with the people
assaulted school and church
with the people
fought feet to feet
beside the people
have given their lives
to the people
but they have forgotten to shout
"i *adore* the people!"

so the people's tribunal approaches.

STREAKING (A PHENOMENON FOLLOWING THE SIXTIES)

the students
went out
of their way
to say
they were not
hurting anyone
or damaging
property
as they streaked across the country—
vulnerable
as a rape victim's
character
after ten years
of public
executions
naked
as the decade
they were formed.

" 'WOMEN OF COLOR' HAVE RARELY HAD THE OPPORTUNITY TO WRITE ABOUT THEIR LOVE AFFAIRS''

(a found poem: The New York Review of Books,
Nov. 30, 1972)

Since he had few intimate friends, and little
is known
about his private life,
it is of interest that Shirley Graham,
his second wife,
has now published an account
of their life together
in *His Truth Is Marching On.*

Unfortunately, however, her version of Du Bois's
career
is perhaps more revealing of herself
than of her late husband.
The gaps in Mrs. Du Bois's memoir
are more instructive
than her recollections.

She has nothing to say
about the internal drama
of the NAACP's birth.
She mentions Du Bois's conflict with

Washington
only in passing
and his debates with
Garvey
             not at all.

Instead she clutters her narrative
with lengthy accounts
of her father's
work
in the NAACP,
the food
   Du Bois liked,
and the international celebrities
she was able to meet
                        because she was married
to Du Bois.

"Women of Color" have rarely had
the opportunity to write about their love
affairs.
There are no black legends comparable to
that of Heloise
and Abelard
or even of Bonnie
and Clyde.

Mrs. Du Bois (who was known as a writer
before she married)
seems to have wanted to fill this gap.

Her recollections, unfortunately, are a cloying
intrusion
into any serious effort
to understand
Du Bois.

She assumes her romance
with Du Bois
to be as interesting as any other aspect
of his career.

FACING THE WAY

the fundamental question about revolution
as lorraine hansberry was not afraid to know
is not simply whether i am willing to give up my life
but if i am prepared to give up my comfort:
clean sheets on my bed
the speed of the dishwasher
and my gas stove
gadgetless
but still preferable to cooking out of doors
over a fire of smoldering roots
my eyes raking the skies for planes
the hills for army tanks.
paintings i have revered stick against my walls
as unconcerned as saints
their perfection alone sufficient for their defense.
yet not one lifeline thrown by the artist
beyond the frame
reaches the boy whose eyes were target
for a soldier's careless aim
or the small girl whose body napalm
a hot bath after mass rape

transformed
or the old women who starve on muscatel
nightly
on the streets of New York.

it is shameful how hard it is for me to give
them up!
to cease this cowardly addiction
to art that transcends time
beauty that nourishes a ravenous spirit
but drags on the mind
whose sale would patch a roof
heat the cold rooms of children. replace an eye.
feed a life.

it does not comfort me now to hear
thepoorweshallhavewithusalways
(Christ should never have said this:
it makes it harder than ever to change)
just as it failed to comfort me
when i was poor.

TALKING TO MY GRANDMOTHER
WHO DIED POOR

(while hearing Richard Nixon declare
"I am not a crook.")

no doubt i will end my life as poor as you
without the wide veranda of your dream
on which to sit and fan myself slowly
without the tall drinks to cool my bored
unthirsty throat.
you will think: Oh, my granddaughter failed
to make something of herself
in the White Man's World!

but i really am not a crook
i am not descended from crooks
my father was not president of anything
and only secretary to the masons
where his dues were a quarter a week
which he did not shirk to pay.

that buys me a new dream
though i may stray
and lust after jewelry
and a small house by the sea:
yet i could give up even lust

in proper times
and open my doors to strangers
or live in one room.
that is the new dream.

in the meantime i hang on
fighting addiction
to the old dream
knowing i must train myself to want
not one bit more
than what i need to keep me alive
working
and recognizing beauty
in your
            so nearly
undefeated face.

JANUARY 10, 1973

i sit for hours staring at my own right hand
wondering if it would help me shoot the judge
who called us chimpanzees from behind his bench
and would it help pour sweet arsenic
into the governor's coffeepot
or drop cyanide into yours.
you don't have to tell me;
i understand these are the clichéd fantasies
of twenty-five million longings
that spring spontaneously to life
every generation.
it is hard for me to write
what everybody already knows;
still, it appears to me
i have pardoned the dead
enough.

FORGIVENESS

YOUR SOUL SHINES

Your soul shines
like the sides of a fish.
My tears are salty
my grief is deep.
Come live in me again.
Each day I walk along the edges
of the tall rocks.

FORGIVENESS

each time I order her to go
for a ruler and face her small
grubby outstretched palm
i feel before hitting it
the sting in my own
and become my mother
preparing to chastise me
on a gloomy Saturday afternoon
long ago. and glaring down into my own sad
and grieving face i forgive myself
for whatever crime i may
have done. as i wish i could always
forgive myself
then as now.

EVEN AS I HOLD YOU

Even as I hold you
I think of you as someone gone
far, far away. Your eyes the color
of pennies in a bowl of dark honey
bringing sweet light to someone else
your black hair slipping through my fingers
is the flash of your head going
around a corner
your smile, breaking before me,
the flippant last turn
of a revolving door,
emptying you out, changed,
away from me.

Even as I hold you
I am letting go.

"GOOD NIGHT, WILLIE LEE, I'LL SEE YOU IN THE MORNING"

Looking down into my father's
dead face
for the last time
my mother said without
tears, without smiles
without regrets
but with *civility*
"Good night, Willie Lee, I'll see you
in the morning."
And it was then I knew that the healing
of all our wounds
is forgiveness
that permits a promise
of our return
at the end.

Horses Make a Landscape Look More Beautiful

In 1978 I moved from Brooklyn, New York, where I'd lived for four years after leaving Mississippi, to northern California. It was one of the best decisions I ever made. My spirit, which had felt so cramped on the East Coast, expanded fully, and I found as many presences to explore within my psyche as I was beginning to recognize in the world.

I could, for the first time, admit and express my grief over the ongoing assassination of the earth, even as I accepted all the parts, good and bad, of my own heritage.

Dedication

for two who
slipped away
almost
entirely:
my "part" Cherokee
great-grandmother
Tallulah
(Grandmama Lula)
on my mother's side
about whom
only one
agreed-upon
thing
is known:
her hair was so long
she could sit on it;

and my white (Anglo-Irish-Scotch?)
great-great-grandfather
on my father's side;
nameless

(Walker, perhaps?),
whose only remembered act
is that he raped
a child:
my great-great-grandmother,
Anne
who bore his son,
my great-grandfather,
Albert
when she was eleven.

Rest in peace.
The meaning of your lives
is still
unfolding.

Rest in peace.
In me
the meaning of your lives
is still
unfolding.

Rest in peace, in me.
The meaning of your lives
is still
unfolding.

Rest. In me
the meaning of your lives
is still
unfolding.

Rest. In peace
in me
the meaning
of our lives
is still
unfolding.

Rest.

We had no word for the strange animal we got from the white man—the horse. So we called it šunka wakan, "holy dog." For bringing us the horse we could almost forgive you for bringing us whiskey. Horses make a landscape look more beautiful.
                              —LAME DEER,
                                   Lame Deer Seeker of Visions

REMEMBER?

Remember me?
I am the girl
with the dark skin
whose shoes are thin
I am the girl
with rotted teeth
I am the dark
rotten-toothed girl
with the wounded eye
and the melted ear.

I am the girl
holding their babies
cooking their meals
sweeping their yards
washing their clothes
Dark and rotting
and wounded, wounded.

I would give
to the human race
only hope.

I am the woman
with the blessed
dark skin
I am the woman
with teeth repaired
I am the woman
with the healing eye
the ear that hears.

I am the woman: Dark,
repaired, healed
Listening to you.

I would give
to the human race
only hope.

I am the woman
offering two flowers
whose roots
are twin

Justice and Hope
Hope and Justice

Let us begin.

THESE MORNINGS
OF RAIN

These mornings of rain
when the house is cozy
and the phone doesn't ring
and I am alone
though snug
in my daughter's
fire-red robe

These mornings of rain
when my lover's large socks
cushion my chilly feet
and meditation
has made me one
with the pine tree
outside my door

These mornings of rain
when all noises coming
from the street
have a slippery sound
and the wind whistles

and I have had my cup
of green tea

These mornings
in Fall
when I have slept late
and dreamed
of people I like
in places where we're
obviously on vacation

These mornings
I do not need
my beloveds' arms about me
until much later
in the day.

I do not need food
I do not need the postperson
I do not need my best friend
to call me
with the latest
on the invasion of Grenada
and her life

I do not need anything.

To be warm, to be dry,
to be writing poems again
(after months of distraction

and emptiness!),
to love and be loved
in absentia
is joy enough for me.

On these blustery mornings
in a city
that could be wet
from my kisses
I need nothing else.

And then again,
I need it all.

FIRST, THEY SAID

First, they said we were savages.
But we knew how well we had treated them
and knew we were not savages.

Then, they said we were immoral.
But we knew minimal clothing
did not equal immoral.

Next, they said our race was inferior.
But we knew our mothers
and we knew our race
was not inferior.

After that, they said we were
a backward people.
But we knew our fathers
and knew we were not backward.

So, then they said we were
obstructing Progress.

But we knew the rhythm of our days
and knew we were not obstructing Progress.

Eventually, they said the truth is that you eat
too much and your villages take up too much
of the land. But we knew we and our children
were starving and our villages were burned
to the ground. So we knew we were not eating
too much or taking up too much of the land.

Finally, they had to agree with us.
They said: You are right. It is not your savagery
or your immorality or your racial inferiority or
your people's backwardness or your obstruction of
Progress or your appetite or your infestation of the land
that is at fault. No. What is at fault
is your existence itself.

Here is money, they said. Raise an army
among your people, and exterminate
yourselves.

In our inferior backwardness
we took the money. Raised an army
among our people.
And now, the people protected, we wait
for the next insulting words
coming out of that mouth.

LISTEN

Listen,
I never dreamed
I would learn to love you so.
You are as flawed
as my vision
As short tempered
as my breath.
Every time you say
you love me
I look for shelter.

But these matters are small.

Lying entranced
by your troubled life
within as without your arms
I am once again
Scholarly.
Studying a way
that is not mine.

Proof of evolution's
variegation.

You would choose
not to come back again,
you say.
Except perhaps
as rock or tree.
But listen, love. Though human,
that is what you are
already
to this student, absorbed.
Human tree and rock already,
to me.

S M

I tell you, Chickadee
I am afraid of people
who cannot cry
Tears left unshed
turn to poison
in the ducts
Ask the next soldier you see
enjoying a massacre
if this is not so.

People who do not cry
are victims
of soul mutilation
paid for in Marlboros
and trucks.

Resist.

Violence does not work
except for the man

who pays your salary
Who knows
if you could still weep
you would not take the job.

THE DIAMONDS ON
LIZ'S BOSOM

The diamonds on Liz's bosom
are not as bright
as his eyes
the morning they took him
to work in the mines
The rubies in Nancy's
jewel box (Oh, how he
loves red!)
not as vivid
as the despair
in his children's
frowns.

Oh, those Africans!

Everywhere you look
they're bleeding
and crying
Crying and bleeding
on some of the whitest necks
in your town.

WE ALONE

We alone can devalue gold
by not caring
if it falls or rises
in the marketplace.
Wherever there is gold
there is a chain, you know,
and if your chain
is gold
so much the worse
for you.

Feathers, shells
and sea-shaped stones
are all as rare.

This could be our revolution:
To love what is plentiful
as much as
what is scarce.

ATTENTIVENESS

When you can no longer
eat
for thinking of those
who starve
is the time to look
beneath the skin
of someone close to you.

Relative, I see the bones
shining
in your face
your hungry eye
prominent as a skull.

I see your dreams
are ashes
that attentiveness alone
does not feed you.

1 9 7 1

I have learned this winter that, yes,
I *am* afraid to die,
even if I do it gently, controlling the rage
myself.
I think of our first week here,
when we bought the rifle to use
against the men
who prowled the street
glowering at this house.
Then it seemed so logical
to shoot to kill. The heart, untroubled;
the head, quite clear of thought.
I dreamed those creatures falling stunned and bloody
across our gleaming floor,
and woke up smiling
at how natural it is
to defend one's life.

(And I will always defend my own, of course.)

But now, I think, although it is natural,
it must continue to be hard;
or "the enemy" becomes the abstraction
he is to those TV faces
we see leering over bodies
they have killed in war. The head on the stick,
the severed ears and genitals
do not conjure up
for mere killers
higher mathematics, the sound of jazz or a baby's fist;
the leer abides.

It is *those* faces, we know,
that should have died.

EVERY MORNING

Every morning I exercise
my body.
It complains
"Why are you doing this to me?"
I give it a plié
in response.
I heave my legs
off the floor
and feel my stomach muscles
rebel:
they are mutinous
there are rumblings
of dissent.

I have other things
to show,
but mostly, my body.
"Don't you see that person
staring at you?" I ask my breasts,
which are still capable
of staring back.

"If I didn't exercise
you couldn't look up
that far.
Your life would be nothing
but shoes."
"Let us at least say we're doing it
for ourselves";
my fingers are eloquent;
they never sweat.

How Poems Are
Made: A
Discredited View

Letting go
in order to hold on
I gradually understand
how poems are made.

There is a place the fear must go.
There is a place the choice must go.
There is a place the loss must go.
The leftover love.
The love that spills out
of the too full cup
and runs and hides
its too full self
in shame.

I gradually comprehend
how poems are made.
To the upbeat flight of memories.
The flagged beats of the running
heart.

I understand how poems are made.
They are the tears
that season the smile.
The stiff-neck laughter
that crowds the throat.
The leftover love.
I know how poems are made.

There is a place the loss must go.
There is a place the gain must go.
The leftover love.

MISSISSIPPI
WINTER I

If I had erased my life there
where the touchdown more than race
holds attention now
how martyred he would have been
his dedication to his work
how unquestionable!
But I am stoned and do not worry
—sitting in this motel room—
for when his footsteps at last disturb
the remnants of my self-pity
there will be nothing here
to point to his love of me
not even my appreciation.

MISSISSIPPI
WINTER II

When you remember me, my child,
be sure to recall that Mama was
a sinner. Her soul was lost
(according to her mama) the very
first time she questioned God. (It
weighed heavily on her, though she
did not like to tell.)
But she wanted to live and what is more
be happy
a concept not understood before the age
of twenty-one.
She was not happy
with fences.

MISSISSIPPI
WINTER III

I cradle my four-year-old daughter
in my arms
alarmed that already she smells
of Love-Is-True perfume.
A present from
her grandmother,
who loves her.
At twenty-nine my own gifts
of seduction
have been squandered. I rise
to Romance
as if it is an Occasional Test
in which my lessons of etiquette
will, thankfully, allow me to fail.

MISSISSIPPI
WINTER IV

My father and mother both
used to warn me
that "a whistling woman and a crowing
hen would surely come to
no good end." And perhaps I should
have listened to them.
But even at the time I knew
that though my end probably might
not
be good
I must whistle
like a woman undaunted
until I reach it.

LOVE IS NOT
CONCERNED

love is not concerned
with whom you pray
or where you slept
the night you ran away
from home
love is concerned
that the beating of your heart
should kill no one.

She said:

She said: "When I was with him,
I used to dream of them together.
Making love to me, he was
making love to her.
That image made me come
every time."

A woman lies alone
outside our door.
I know she dreams us
making love;
you inside me,
her lips on my breasts.

WALKER

When I no longer have your heart
I will not request your body
your presence
or even your polite conversation.
I will go away to a far country
separated from you by the sea
—on which I cannot walk—
and refrain even from sending
letters
describing my pain.

KILLERS

With their money they bought ignorance
and killed the dreamer.
But you, Chenault,* have killed
the dreamer's mother.
They tell me you smile happily
on TV,
mission "half-accomplished."

I can no longer observe such pleased mad
faces.
The mending heart breaks
to break again.

*The assassin of Martin Luther King, Jr.'s mother, Mrs. Alberta King. His
plan had been to murder Martin Luther King, Sr., as well.

SONGLESS

What is the point
of being artists
if we cannot save our life?
That is the cry
that wakes us
in our sleep.
Being happy is not the only
happiness.
And how many gadgets
can one person manage
at one time?

Over in the Other World
the women count
their wealth
in empty
calabashes.
How to transport
food
from watering hole
to watering

hole
has ceased to be
a problem
since the animals
died
and seed grain shrunk
to fit the pocket.

Now
it is just a matter
of who can create
the finest
decorations
on the empty
pots.

They say in Nicaragua
the whole
government
writes,
makes music
and paints,
saving their own
and helping the people save
their own lives.

(I ask you to notice
who, songless,
rules us
here.)

They say in Nicaragua
the whole
government
writes
and makes
music
saving its own
and helping the people save
their own lives.

These are not containers
void of food.
These are not decorations
on empty pots.

A FEW SIRENS

Today I am at home
writing poems.
My life goes well:
only a few sirens herald disaster
in the ghetto
down the street.
In the world, people die
of hunger.
On my block we lose
jobs, housing and breasts.
But in the world
children are lost;
whole countries of children
starved to death
before the age
of five
each year;
their mothers squatted
in the filth
around the empty cooking pot
wondering:

But I cannot pretend
to know
what they wonder.
A walled horror
instead of thought
would be my mind.

And our children
gladly starve themselves.

Thinking of the food I eat
every day
I want to vomit, like
people who throw up
at will,
understanding that whether
they digest or not
they must consume.

Can you imagine?

Rather than let the hungry
inside the restaurants
Let them eat vomit, they say.
They are applauded
for this. For this
they are light.

But
wasn't there a time
when food was sacred?

When a dead child
starved naked
among the oranges
in the marketplace
spoiled
the appetite?

POEM AT
THIRTY-NINE

How I miss my father.
I wish he had not been
so tired
when I was
born.

Writing deposit slips and checks
I think of him.
He taught me how.
This is the form,
he must have said:
the way it is done.
I learned to see
bits of paper
as a way
to escape
the life he knew
and even in high school
had a savings
account.

He taught me
that telling the truth
did not always mean
a beating;
though many of my truths
must have grieved him
before the end.

How I miss my father!
He cooked like a person
dancing
in a yoga meditation
and craved the voluptuous
sharing
of good food.

Now I look and cook just like him:
my brain light;
tossing this and that
into the pot;
seasoning none of my life
the same way twice; happy to feed
whoever strays my way.

He would have grown
to admire
the woman I've become:
cooking, writing, chopping wood,
staring into the fire.

I Said to
Poetry

I said to Poetry: "I'm finished
with you."
Having to almost die
before some weird light
comes creeping through
is no fun.
"No thank you, Creation,
no muse need apply.
I'm out for good times—
at the very least,
some painless convention."

Poetry laid back
and played dead
until this morning.
I wasn't sad or anything,
only restless.

Poetry said: "You remember
the desert, and how glad you were
that you have an eye

to see it with? You remember
that, if ever so slightly?"
I said: "I didn't hear that.
Besides, it's five o'clock in the a.m.
I'm not getting up
in the dark
to talk to you."

Poetry said: "But think about the time
you saw the moon
over that small canyon
that you liked much better
than the grand one—and how surprised you were
that the moonlight was green
and you still had
one good eye
to see it with.

Think of that!"

"I'll join the church!" I said,
huffily, turning my face to the wall.
"I'll learn how to pray again!"

"Let me ask you," said Poetry.
"When you pray, what do you think
you'll see?"

Poetry had me.

"There's no paper
in this room," I said.
"And that new pen I bought
makes a funny noise."

"Bullshit," said Poetry.
"Bullshit," said I.

GRAY

I have a friend
who is turning gray,
not just her hair,
and I do not know
why this is so.

Is it a lack of vitamin E
pantothenic acid, or B-12?
Or is it from being frantic
and alone?

"How long does it take you to love someone?"
I ask her.
"A hot second," she replies.
"And how long do you love them?"
"Oh, anywhere up to several months."
"And how long does it take you
to get over loving them?"
"Three weeks," she said, "tops."

Did I mention I am also
turning gray?
It is because I *adore* this woman
who thinks of love
in this way.

OVERNIGHTS

Staying overnight in a friend's house
I miss my own bed
in San Francisco
and the man in my bed
but mostly just
my bed
It's a mattress on the floor
but so what?

This bed I'm in is lumpy
It lists to one side
It has thin covers
and is short

All night I toss and turn
dreaming of my bed
in San Francisco
with me in it
and the man too sometimes
in it
but together

Sometimes we are eating pastrami
which he likes
Sometimes we are eating
Other things

My Daughter Is Coming!

My daughter is coming!
I have bought her a bed
and a chair
a mirror, a lamp
and a desk.
Her room is all ready
except that the curtains
are torn.
Do I have time to buy shoji panels
for the window?
I do not.

First I must WRITE A SPEECH
see the doctor about my tonsils
which are dying ahead of schedule
see the barber and do a wash
cross the country
cross Brooklyn and Manhattan
MAKE A SPEECH
READ A POEM
liberate my daughter

from her father and Washington, D.C.
recross the country
and present her to her room.

My daughter is coming!

Will she like her bed,
her chair, her mirror
desk and lamp

Or will she see only
the torn curtains?

WHEN GOLDA MEIR
WAS IN AFRICA

When Golda Meir
was in Africa
she shook out her hair
and combed it
everywhere she went.

According to her autobiography
Africans loved this.

In Russia, Minneapolis, London, Washington, D.C.
Germany, Palestine, Tel Aviv and
Jerusalem
she never combed at all.
There was no point. In those
places people said, "She looks like
any other aging grandmother. She looks
like a troll. Let's sell her cookery
and guns."

"*Kreplach* your cookery," said Golda.

Only in Africa could she finally
settle down and comb her hair.
The children crept up and stroked it,
and she felt beautiful.

Such wonderful people, Africans
Childish, arrogant, self-indulgent, pompous,
cowardly and treacherous—a *great* disappointment
to Israel, of course, and really rather
ridiculous in international affairs,
but, withal, opined Golda, a people of charm
and good taste.

If "Those People"
Like You

If "those people" like you
it is a bad sign.
It is the kiss of death.
This is the kind of thing we discuss
among ourselves.

We were about to throw out
a perfectly good man.

"They are always telling me
I've got to meet him! They
are always saying how superior
he is! And those who cannot
say he's superior say 'How *Nice*.'
Well! We know what this means.
The man's insufferable. *They're*
insufferable. How can he stand
them, if he means any good to us?"

It so happened I knew this man.
"You've got to meet him," I said.

"He *is* superior, nice, and not at all
insufferable." And this is true.

But the talk continued:
If "those people" like you
it is a bad sign.
It is the kiss of death.
Because that is the kind of thing
we talk about
among ourselves.

On Sight

I am so thankful I have seen
The Desert
And the creatures in The Desert
And the desert Itself.

The Desert has its own moon
Which I have seen
With my own eye

There is no flag on it.

Trees of the desert have arms
All of which are always up
That is because the moon is up
The sun is up
Also the sky
The stars

Clouds
None with flags.

If there were flags, I doubt
The trees would point.
Would you?

I'M REALLY
VERY FOND

I'm really very fond of you,
he said.

I don't like fond.
It sounds like something
you would tell a dog.

Give me love,
or nothing.

Throw your fond in a pond,
I said.

But what I felt for him
was also warm, frisky,
moist-mouthed,
eager,
and could swim away

if forced to do so.

Representing
the Universe

There are five people in this room
who still don't know what I'm saying.
"What is she saying?" they're asking.
"What is she doing here?"

It is not enough to be interminable;
one must also be precise.

The Wasichus* did not kill them to eat; they killed them for the metal that makes them crazy, and they took only the hides to sell. Sometimes they did not even take the hides, only the tongues; and I have heard that fire-boats came down the Missouri River loaded with dried bison tongues. . . . And when there was nothing left but heaps of bones, the Wasichus came and gathered up even the bones and sold them.

—BLACK ELK,
Black Elk Speaks

*Wasichu in Sioux means "he who takes the fat."

FAMILY OF

Sometimes I feel so bad
I ask myself
Who in the world
Have I murdered?

It is a Wasichu's voice
That asks this question,
Coming from nearly inside of me.

It is asking to be let in, of course.

I am here too! he shouts,
Shaking his fist.
Pay some attention to me!

But if I let him in
What a mess he'll make!
Even now asking who
He's murdered!
Next he'll complain
Because we don't keep a maid!

He is murderous and lazy
And I fear him,
This small, white man;
Who would be neither courteous
Nor clean
Without my help.
By the hour I linger
On his deficiencies
And his unfortunate disposition,
Keeping him sulking
And kicking
At the door.

There is the mind that creates
Without loving, for instance,
The childish greed;
The boatloads and boatloads
of tongues . . .

Besides, where would he fit
If I did let him in?
No sitting at round tables
For him!

I could be a liberal
And admit one of his children;
Or be a radical and permit two.
But it is *he* asking
To be let in, alas.

Our mothers learned to receive him occasionally,
Passing as Christ. But this did not help us much.
Or perhaps it made all the difference.

But there. He is bewildered
And tuckered out with the waiting.
He's giving up and going away
Until the next time.

And murdered quite sufficiently, too, I think,
Until the next time.

Each One, Pull One

(Thinking of Lorraine Hansberry)

We must say it all, and as clearly
as we can. For, even before we are dead,
they are busy
trying to bury us.

Were we black? Were we women? Were we gay?
Were we the wrong *shade* of black? Were we yellow?
Did we, God forbid, love the wrong person, country
or politics? Were we Agnes Smedley or John Brown?

But, most of all, did we write exactly what we saw,
as clearly as we could? Were we unsophisticated
enough to cry *and* scream?

Well, then, they will fill our eyes,
our ears, our noses and our mouths
with the mud
of oblivion. They will chew up
our fingers in the night. They will pick
their teeth with our pens. They will sabotage

both our children
and our art.

Because when we show what we see,
they will discern the inevitable:
We do not worship them.

We do not worship them.
We do not worship what they have made.
We do not trust them.
We do not believe what they say.
We do not love their efficiency.
Or their power plants.
We do not love their factories.
Or their smog.
We do not love their television programs.
Or their radioactive leaks.
We find their papers boring.
We do not worship their cars.
We do not worship their blondes.
We do not envy their penises.
We do not think much
of their Renaissance.
We are indifferent to England.
We have grave doubts about their brains.

In short, we who write, paint, sculpt, dance
or sing
share the intelligence and thus the fate
of all our people

in this land.
We are not different from them,
neither above nor below,
outside nor inside.
We are the same.
And we do not worship them.

We do not worship them.
We do not worship their movies.
We do not worship their songs.
We do not think their newscasts
cast the news.
We do not admire their president.
We know why the White House is white.
We do not find their children irresistible;
We do not agree they should inherit the earth.

But lately you have begun to help them
bury us. You who said: King was just a womanizer;
Malcom, just a thug; Sojourner, folksy; Hansberry,
a traitor (or whore, depending); Fannie Lou Hamer,
merely spunky; Zora Hurston, Nella Larsen, Toomer:
reactionary, brainwashed, spoiled by whitefolks, minor;
Agnes Smedley, a spy.

I look into your eyes;
you are throwing in the dirt.
You, standing in the grave
with me. Stop it!

Each one must pull one.

Look, I, temporarily on the rim
of the grave,
have grasped my mother's hand
my father's leg.
There is the hand of Robeson
Langston's thigh
Zora's arm and hair
your grandfather's lifted chin
the lynched woman's elbow
what you've tried to forget
of your grandmother's frown.

Each one, pull one back into the sun

We who have stood over
so many graves
know that no matter what *they* do
all of us must live
or none.

WHO?

Who has not been
invaded
by the Wasichu?

Not I, said the people.

Not I, said the trees.

Not I, said the waters.

Not I, said the rocks.

Not I, said the air.

Moon!

We hoped
you were safe.

WITHOUT
COMMERCIALS

Listen,
stop tanning yourself
and talking about
fishbelly
white.
The color white
is not bad at all.
There are white mornings
that bring us days.
Or, if you must,
tan only because
it makes you happy
to be brown,
to be able to see
for a summer
the whole world's
darker
face
reflected
in your own.

*

Stop unfolding
your eyes.
Your eyes are
beautiful.
Sometimes
seeing you in the street
the fold zany
and unexpected
I want to kiss
them
and usually
it is only
old
gorgeous
black people's eyes
I want
to kiss.

* *

Stop trimming
your nose.
When you
diminish
your nose
your songs
become little
tinny, muted
and snub.
Better you should
have a nose
impertinent

as a flower,
sensitive
as a root;
wise, elegant,
serious and deep.
A nose that
sniffs
the essence
of Earth. And knows
the message
of every
leaf.

* * *

Stop bleaching
your skin
and talking
about
so much black
is not beautiful
The color black
is not bad
at all.
There are black nights
that rock
us
in dreams.
Or, if you must,
bleach only
because it pleases you
to be brown,

to be able to see
for as long
as you can bear it
the whole world's
lighter face
reflected
in your own.

* * * *

As for me,
I have learned
to worship
the sun
again.
To affirm
the adventures
of hair.

For we are all
splendid
descendants
of Wilderness,
Eden:
needing only
to see
each other
without
commercials
to believe.

Copied skillfully
as Adam.

Original

as Eve.

No One Can Watch the Wasichu

No one can watch
the Wasichu
anymore
He is always
penetrating
a people
whose country
is too small
for him
His bazooka
always
sticking up
from some
howling
mother's
backyard.

No one can watch
the Wasichu
anymore
He is always

squashing
something
Somebody's guts
trailing
his shoe.

No one can watch
the Wasichu
anymore
He is scalping
the earth
till she runs
into the ocean
The dust of her
flight
searing
our sight.

No one can watch
the Wasichu
anymore
Smirking
into our bedrooms
with his
terrible
Nightly News . . .

No one can watch
the Wasichu
anymore.

Regardless.

He has filled

Our every window
with
his face.

The Thing Itself

Now I am going
to rape you,
you joked;
after a pleasure
wrung
from me.

With playful roughness
you dragged my body
to meet yours;
on your face
the look of
mock
lust
you think
all real women
like

As all "real" women
really
like rape.

Lying
barely breathing
beneath
your heaving
heaviness
I fancied I saw
my great-great-grandmother's
small hands
encirle
your pale neck.

There was no
pornography
in her world
from which to learn
to relish the pain.

(She was the thing
itself.)

Oh, you who seemed
the best of them,
my own sad
Wasichu;
in what gibberish
was our freedom
engraved on
our chains.

TORTURE

When they torture your mother
plant a tree
When they torture your father
plant a tree
When they torture your brother
and your sister
plant a tree
When they assassinate
your leaders
and lovers
plant a tree
When they torture you
too bad
to talk
plant a tree.

When they begin to torture
the trees
and cut down the forest
they have made
start another.

WELL.

Well.

He was a poet
a priest
a revolutionary
compañero
and we were right
to be seduced.

He brought us greetings
from his countrypeople
and informed us
with lifted
fist
that they would not
be moved.

All his poems
were eloquent.

I liked
especially
the one
that said
the revolution
must
liberate
the cougars, the trees,
and the lakes;
when he read it
everyone
breathed
relief;
ecology
lives
of all places
in Central
America!
we thought.

And then he read
a poem
about Grenada
and we
smiled
until he began
to describe
the women:

Well. One woman
when she smiled
had shiny black
lips
which reminded him
of black legs
(vaselined, no doubt),
her whole mouth
to the poet
revolutionary
suddenly
a leg
(and one said
What?)

Another one,
duly noted by
the priest,
apparently
barely attentive
at a political
rally
eating
a mango

Another wears
a red dress,
her breasts
(no kidding!)
like coconuts. . . .

Well. Nobody ever said
supporting other people's revolutions
wouldn't make us
ill:

But what a pity
that
the poet
the priest
and the revolution
never seem
to arrive
for the black woman,
herself.

Only for her black lips
or her black leg
does one or the other
arrive:
only for her
devouring mouth
always depicted
in the act
of eating
something colorful

only for her breasts
like coconuts
and her red dress.

SONG

The world is full of colored
people
People of Color
Tra-la-la
The world is full of
colored people
Tra-la-la-la-la.

They have black hair
and black and brown
eyes
The world is full of
colored people
Tra-la-la.

The world is full of colored
people
People of Color
Tra-la-la

The world is full of colored
people
Tra-la-la-la-la.

Their skins are pink and yellow
and brown
All colored people
People of Color
Colored people
Tra-la-la.

Some have full lips
Some have thin
Full of colored people
People of Color
Colored lips
Tra-la-la.

The world is full of
colored people
People of Color
Colorful people
Tra-la-la!

THESE DAYS

Some words for people I think of as friends.

These days I think of Belvie
swimming happily in the country pond
coating her face with its mud.
She says:
"We could put the whole bottom of this pond in jars
and sell it to the folks
in the city!"
Lying in the sun she dreams
of making our fortune, à la Helena Rubenstein.
Bottling the murky water
too smelly to drink,
offering exotic mud facials and mineral baths
at exorbitant fees.
But mostly she lies in the sun
dreaming of water, sun and the earth
itself—

Surely the earth can be saved for Belvie.

These days I think of Robert
folding his child's tiny shirts

consuming TV dinners ("A kind of *processed* flavor")
rushing off each morning to school—then to the office,
the supermarket, the inevitable meeting: writing,
speaking, marching against oppression, hunger,
ignorance.
And in between having a love affair
with tiny wildflowers and gigantic
rocks.
"Look at this one!" he cries,
as a small purple face
raises its blue eye to the sun.
"Wow, look at that one!" he says,
as we pass a large rock
reclining beside the road.
He is the man with child
the new old man.
Brushing hair, checking hands, nails
and teeth.
A sick child finds comfort
lying on his chest all night
as do I.

Surely the earth can be saved for Robert.

These days I think of Elena.
In the summers, for years, she camps
beside the Northern rivers
sometimes with her children
sometimes with women friends
from "way, way back."

She is never too busy to *want* at least
to join a demonstration
or to long to sit
beside
a river.
"I will not think less of you
if you do *not* attend this meeting," she says,
making us compañeras for life.

Surely the earth can be saved for Elena.

These days I think of Susan;
so many of her people lost
in the Holocaust. Every time I see her
I can't believe it.
"You have to have some of my cosmos seeds!"
she says
over the phone. "The blooms
are glorious!"
Whenever we are together
we eat a lot.
If I am at her house
it is bacon, boiled potatoes,
coffee and broiled fish:
if she is at my house it is
oyster stew, clams, artichokes
and wine.
Our dream is for time in which
to walk miles together, a couple
of weeds stuck between our teeth,

comfy in our yogi pants
discoursing on Woolf
and child raising,
essay writing and gardening.
Susan makes me happy
because she exists.

Surely the earth can be saved for Susan.

These days I think of Sheila.
" 'Sheila' is already a spiritual name," she says.
And "Try meditation and jogging both."
When we are together we talk
and talk
about The Spirit
About What is Good and What is Not.
There was a time she applauded my anger,
now she feels it is something I should outgrow.
"It is not a useful emotion," she says. "And besides,
if you think about it, there's nothing worth
getting angry about."
"I do not like anger," I say.
"It raises my blood pressure.
I do not like violence. So much has been done to me.
But having embraced my complete being
I find anger
and the capacity for violence
within me.
Control
rather than eradication

is about the best
I feel I can do.
Besides, they intend to murder us,
you know."
"Yes, I understand," she says.
"But try meditation
and jogging *both*;
you'll be surprised how calm you feel."
I meditate, walk briskly, and take deep, deep breaths
for I know the importance of peace to the inner self.
When I talk to Sheila
I am forced to honor
my own ideals.

Surely the earth can be saved for Sheila.

These days I think of Gloria.
"The mere *sight* of an airplane puts me to sleep,"
she says.
Since she is not the pilot, this makes sense.
If this were a courageous country,
it would ask Gloria to lead it
since she is sane and funny and beautiful and smart
and the National Leaders we've always had
are not.
When I listen to her talk about women's rights
children's rights
men's rights
I think of the long line of Americans
who should have been president, but weren't.

Imagine Crazy Horse as president. Sojourner Truth.
John Brown. Harriet Tubman. Black Elk or Geronimo.
Imagine President Martin Luther King confronting
the youthful "Oppie" Oppenheimer. Imagine President
Malcolm X going after the Klan. Imagine President Stevie
Wonder dealing with the "Truly Needy."
Imagine President Shirley Chisholm, Ron Dellums or
Sweet Honey in the Rock
dealing with Anything.
It is imagining to make us weep with frustration,
as we languish under real estate dealers, killers,
and bad actors.

Gloria makes me aware of how much we lose by denying,
exiling or repressing parts of ourselves
so that other parts,
grotesque and finally lethal
may creep into the light.
"Women must seize the sources of reproduction," she says,
knowing her Marx and her Sanger too.

Surely the earth can be saved for Gloria.

These days I think of Jan,
who makes the most exquisite goblets
—and plates and casseroles.
Her warm hands steady on the cool
and lively clay,
her body attentive and sure, bending over the wheel.
I could watch her work for hours—

but there is never time. On one visit I see the bags
of clay. The next visit, I see pale and dusty molds,
odd pieces of hardening handles and lids. On another,
I see a stacked kiln. On another, magical objects of use
splashed with blue, streaked with black and red.
She sits quietly beside her creations
at countless fairs
watching without nostalgia
their journeys into the world.
She makes me consider how long
people have been making things. How wise
and thoughtful people often are.
A world without Jan would be like her house
when she is someplace else—gray, and full of furniture
I've never seen before.

Our dream is to sit on a ridge top for days
and reminisce
about the anti-nuke movement.
The time we were together
at a woman's music festival, and Diablo Canyon
called her.
The more comic aspects
of her arrest.

There is a way that she says "um *hum*" that means a lot
to me.

Surely the earth can be saved for Jan.

These days I think of Rebecca.
"Mama, are you a racist?" she asks.
And I realize I have badmouthed white people
once too often
in her presence.

Years ago I would have wondered
how white people have managed to live
all these years
with this question
from their children;
or, how did they train their children
not to ask?

Now I think how anti-racism
like civil rights or
affirmative action
helps white people too.
Even if they are killing us
we have to say, to try to believe,
it is the way they are raised,
not genetics,
that causes their bizarre,
death-worshiping
behavior.

"If we were raised like white people,
to think we are superior to everything else
God made, we too would behave the way
they do," say the elders.

And: "White folks could *be* people of color
if they'd only relax."

Besides, my daughter declares
her own white father "Good," and reminds me
it is often black men
who menace us on
the street.

Talking to Rebecca about race almost always
guarantees a headache.
But that is a small price
for the insight and clarity
she brings.

Surely the earth can be saved for Rebecca.

These days I think of John, Yoko and Sean Lennon.
Whenever I listen
to "Working-Class Hero,"
I laugh: because John says "fucking"
twice,
and it is always a surprise
though I know the record by heart.
I like to imagine
him putting Sean to bed

or exchanging his own hard,
ass-kicking boots
for sneakers.

I like to imagine Yoko
making this white boy deal with the word NO
for the first time.
And the word YES forever.
I like to think of this brave
and honest
new age family
that dared to sing itself
even as anger, fear, sadness and death
squeezed its vocal cords.

Yoko knows the sounds of a woman coming
are finer by far than those of a B-52
on a bombing raid.

And a Kotex plastered across
a man's forehead at dinner
can indicate serenity.

> *Hold on world*
> *World hold on*
> *It's gonna be all right*
> *You gonna see the light*
> *(Ohh) when you're one*
> *Really one*
> *You get things done*
> *Like they never been done*
> *So hold on.**

*From "Hold On John," by John Lennon.

Surely the earth can be saved
by all the people
who insist
on love.

Surely the earth can be saved for us.

We Have a
Beautiful Mother:
Previously
Uncollected Poems

For most of the years I have been writing poetry I have envied musicians. Only musicians, it seemed to me, were always at one with their creations. But lately I see that poetry, too, is inseparable from the heart and soul from which it comes. And that there is only waiting for poetry, there is no solicitation. When it comes I recognize it as grace, and am overwhelmed with gratitude, *and when it does not come I find it has left me with this attitude about life. Poetry, I have discovered, is always unexpected and always as faithful and honest as dreams.*

*In memory of my father
who, somber,
left me
his smile.*

*(Proving magic survives
even under patriarchy.)*

MY HEART HAS REOPENED TO YOU

The Place Where I Was Born

I am a displaced person. I sit here on a swing on the deck of my house in Northern California admiring how the fog has turned the valley below into a lake. For hours nothing will be visible below me except this large expanse of vapor; then slowly, as the sun rises and gains in intensity, the fog will start to curl up and begin its slow rolling drift toward the ocean. People here call it the dragon; and, indeed, a dragon is what it looks like, puffing and coiling, winged, flaring and in places thin and discreet, as it races before the sun, back to its ocean coast den. Mornings I sit here in awe and great peace. The mountains across the valley come and go in the mist; the redwoods and firs, oaks and giant bays appear as clumpish spires, enigmatic shapes of green, like the stone forests one sees in Chinese paintings of Guilin.

It is incredibly beautiful where I live. Not fancy at all, or exclusive. But from where I sit on my deck I can look down on the backs of hawks, and the wide, satiny wings of turkey vultures glistening in the sun become my present connection to ancient Egyptian Africa. The pond is so still below me that the trees reflected in it seem, from this distance, to be painted in its depths.

All this: the beauty, the quiet, the cleanliness, the peace, is what I love. I realize how lucky I am to have found it here. And yet, there are days when my view of the mountains and redwoods makes me nostalgic for small rounded hills easily walked over, and for the look of big leaf poplar and the scent of pine.

I am nostalgic for the land of my birth, the land I left forever when I was thirteen—moving first to the town of Eatonton, and then, at seventeen, to the city of Atlanta.

I cried one day as I talked to a friend about a tree I loved as a child. A tree that had sheltered my father on his long cold walk to school each morning: it was midway between his house and the school and because there was a large cavity in its trunk, a fire could be made inside it. During my childhood, in a tiny, overcrowded house in a tiny dell below it, I looked up at it frequently and felt reassured by its age, its generosity despite its years of brutalization (the fires, I knew, had to hurt), and its tall, old-growth pine nobility. When it was struck by lightning and killed, and then was cut down and made into firewood, I grieved as if it had been a person. Secretly. Because who among the members of my family would not have laughed at my grief?

I have felt entirely fortunate to have had this companion, and even today remember it with gratitude. But why the tears? my friend wanted to know. And it suddenly dawned on me that perhaps it *was* sad that it was a tree and not a member of my family to whom I was so emotionally close.

*

As a child I assumed I would always have the middle Georgia landscape to live in, as Brer Rabbit, a native also, and relative, had his brier patch. It was not to be. The pain of racist oppression, and its consequence, economic impoverishment, drove me to the four corners of the earth in search of justice and peace, and work that affirmed my whole being. I have come to rest here, weary from travel, on a deck—not a southern front porch—overlooking another world.

I am content; and yet, I wonder what my life would have been like if I had been able to stay home?

I remember early morning fogs in Georgia, not so dramatic as California ones, but magical too because out of the Southern fog of memory tramps my dark father, smiling and large, glowing with rootedness, and talking of hound dogs, biscuits and coons. And my equally rooted mother bustles around the corner of our house preparing to start a wash, the fire under the black wash pot extending a circle of warmth in which I, a grave-eyed child, stand. There is my sister Ruth, beautiful to me and dressed elegantly for high school in gray felt skirt and rhinestone brooch, hurrying up the road to catch the yellow school bus which glows like a large glow worm in the early morning fog.

O, landscape of my birth
because you were so good to me as I grew
I could not bear to lose you.
O, landscape of my birth
because when I lost you, a part of my soul died.
O, landscape of my birth

because to save myself I pretended it was *you*
who died.
        You that now did not exist
because I could not see you.
        But O, landscape of my birth
now I can confess how I have lied.
        Now I can confess the sorrow
of my heart
        as the tears flow
and I see again with memory's bright eye
my dearest companion cut down
and can bear to resee myself
so lonely and so small
there in the sunny meadows
and shaded woods
of childhood
where my crushed spirit
and stricken heart
ran in circles
looking for a friend.

Soon I will have known fifty summers.
Perhaps that is why
my heart
an imprisoned tree
so long clutched tight
inside its core
insists
on shedding
like iron leaves

the bars
from its cell.

You flow into me.
And like the Aborigine or Bushperson or Cherokee
who braves everything
to stumble home to die
no matter that cowboys
are herding cattle where the ancestors slept
I return to you, my earliest love.

Weeping in recognition at the first trees
I ever saw, the first hills I ever climbed and rested my
    unbearable cares
upon, the first rivers I ever dreamed myself across,
the first pebbles I ever lifted up, warm from the sun, and
    put into
my mouth.

    O landscape of my birth
you have never been far from my heart.
It is *I* who have been far.
    If you will take me back
    Know that I
    Am yours.

SOME
THINGS I LIKE ABOUT
MY TRIPLE BLOODS

Black relatives
you are always
putting yourselves
down
But you almost never
put down
Africa
You are the last
man
woman
and child
to stand up
for everybody's
Mother
though so much rampant motherfuckering in the language
    makes one
blue
And I like that
about you.

White relatives
I like your roads

of course you make
too many of them
and a lot of them
aren't going anywhere
but you make them really well
nevertheless
as if you know where they go and how they'll do
And I like that
about you.

Red relatives
you never start
anything
on time
Time itself
in your thought
not being about
timeliness
so much
as about
time*less*ness.
Powwows could
take forever
and probably do
in your view
and you could care
less.
And I like that
about you.

TELLING

I want to be with you
in the pain and sadness
or relief, of abortion
in the pain and joy
or horror, of birth.

Through my words
little sister
I am taking your hand in mine.
I am telling you
you will never
again
be alone.

Is solace anywhere
more comforting
than in the arms
of sisters?
Words flung like warm flames
across

inner continents
of ice and glass.

And when you die
please know
I will have gone ahead
to pick out the best place.

To say Welcome.

Sit here beside me, my love
and let heaven be heaven
at last.

PAGAN

for Muriel Rukeyser

At home
in the countryside
I make the decision
to leave your book
—overdue at the library—
face up, "promiscuous"
out in the sun.

Pagan.

I laugh to see
this was our religion
all along.

Hidden
even from ourselves
taught
early
not to touch
the earth.

Years of white gloves
straight seamed hose.
"Being good girls."
Scripture like chains.
Dogma like flies.
Smiles like locks
and lies.

NATURAL STAR

I am in mourning
for your face
The one I used to love
to see ´
Leaping, glowing
upon the stage
The mike
eager . . .
Thrusting
in your fist.

I am in mourning
for your face
the shining eyes
the happy teeth
the look that said
I *am* the world
and aren't you
glad
Not to mention
deeply
in luck.

I am in mourning
for the sweet brown innocence
of your skin
your perfect nose
the shy smile
that lit you
like a light.

I am in mourning
for a face
the Universe
in its goodness
makes but once
each
thousand
years
     and smiles
and sends it out
to spread great joy
Itself well pleased.

I am in mourning
for your beloved face
so thoroughly and
undeservedly released.

Oh, my pretty little
brother. Genius. Child.
Sing to us. Dance.

Rest in peace.

IF THERE WAS ANY JUSTICE

If there was any justice
in the world

I'd own
Van Gogh's
starry night.
Not the tall
linear one
I have
always
coveted
but the wide
horizontal one
on which the paint
is desperate
praise.

It would hang
over the headboard
of my bed
so that

every night
before falling
asleep
I could look at it
and then above
it
through the skylight
at the heavens.

If there was any justice
in the world
I could have saved up
for it
and bought it
for the cost
of a fancy dress
or a modest
house.

Vincent
would have wanted me
to have it. Of this
I have no doubt.

How he would smile
to see how   every night
I journeyed
through the cosmos
on the wings
of his brush.

My dreadlocks
connecting canvas to
moon.

He probably
would have given
me
the painting
if we had been
neighbors
friends
or
bar room
aficionados
and I had offered
him a watermelon
or homemade
wine.

If there was any justice
in the world
I'd also have
that last
painting he did
of the reaper
and the
wide field
of wheat
and the crows.

I'd have the
Sunflowers.
All of them
of course.

Whoever
has the
poor taste
to hoard them
could keep the
ugly portraits
of Madame Whosis
& Dr. Whatsis
but there are
a couple
of garden scenes
I would also
take.

Vincent
knowing I
value flowers
& orderly
disarray
would have wanted
them
to be mine.

If we had met
in the presence

of these
paintings
he couldn't have missed
the wonder
the reverence
the stark
recognition
of shared Life
in my eyes.

My delight in him
spirit   eye
& hand.

As the world
rushes madly
to its end
and one imagines
the *Starry Night*
lonely
as Vincent
himself
in its vault
bursting
suddenly
into flame
like a bit of
star
or a bit
of rubbish.

And the same
tired assassins
whose blindness
drove him
insane
seeking at last
to destroy
all
the beauty
beyond
the vault
that
he labored
so
to make
them see
&
seeing

save.

BEAST

Whenever I do not create
I feel like a beast.
A beast they say
is a being
who
through horror
and impoverishment
loses its soul.

Earth
I beg of you
a beast
in the making
to reclaim
creation
as a rolling over
of the soul.
The absolute
wilful,
self-assurance

that there is
no lack.

I beg of you
rise again.
Shake the concrete
off your back.

NDEBELE

Looking into your eyes
I can see why
they are always
trying
to murder you.

No matter how much
they take
from you
you still have more.

It is in the carriage
of your head
the grace of your neck
It is in your walk
the way you do
or do not smile.

Seeing you there
among your children
and your art

knowing they have stripped
from you
all but barest life
they must think
the Great Spirit
did indeed
pass them by.

They eat and eat
the food they steal
from you;
it only makes them
gross.

They wear and wear
the clothes
they steal from you
they are more naked
than before.

They rape and praise
the land they steal
from you
it poisons them.

"If we do not
carry on our
traditions
the ancestors
may think

we are Sotho
—or even white
people," you exclaim.
Painting a whole
house
with just
your fingertips.

Their envy of us
has always been
our greatest crime.

What are we to do?
African women,
we insist
on all the
freedoms . . .
Ours the privilege
of not even
comprehending
what it means
to give up.

Far into the night
years and days
without your man

Your brothers, your sons
dying on the long
bus rides

to Pretoria's
mines
You paint. You sculpt.
You make beaded
everythings.

There is a scepter
you cover in beads
that you explain
to strangers
is really
a telephone pole.

They crush and crush
your heart;
your humor
escapes.

WE HAVE A MAP
OF THE WORLD

*In honor of Soviet poet Olzhas Suleimenov, Native Kazakstanan,
and the Nevada-Semipalatinsk Anti-Nuclear Movement*

> *"We have a map*
> *of the world*
> *showing how*
> *all nuclear tests*
> *have been*
> *conducted*
> *on the territory*
> *of Native*
> *peoples."*
>
> > Raymond Yowell
> > Western Shoshone National Council
> > Las Vegas, Nevada, October 21, 1988

As it is
in my country
so it is
in yours.

I look into
your Asian
your Indian

eyes
and read
your fear:

that your cows
eat
poisoned
grass:

that your wheat
kills:
that your children
shrink
from contact
with Mother's
milk.

It is all known
now.
The darkness
at the heart
of the light.

Even by those
afraid to know
their country's
secrets.
Even by those
who deadened themselves

to keep
from finding out.

The old men
show
their power
by exploding
weapons
deadly seed
deep inside
the body
of the earth.

They grunt
that they see God
in the flash
that blinds
them
and us.

They tell us
such vigorous rape
as theirs
will keep
our countries
young.

But we
are not fooled.

We see
sometimes unbelieving
that our days
have become brutish
and short.

We see
sometimes
uncomprehending
that our pain
and our deaths
are long.

We feel
the heavy trauma
of kissing
of making love
under a cloud
of radioactive dust.

O poets
singers
and children
of the world
unite.
Lift every
voice
and sing
out
against the old men

who hate us
hate themselves
and hate
the earth.

The old men
to whom
natural
fucking
is a thing
of the past.
And somebody else's past
at that.

Who strangle
our orgasms
with the wickedness
of their advances.

Who hang our babies
with the promise
of their words.

Who asphyxiate
our hopes
with the scratch
of a pen.

The old paleheart vampires
sucking up the world.

The old men
who ejaculate
plutonium.

The old men
who give us
blood
to drink.

THE RIGHT TO LIFE: WHAT CAN THE WHITE MAN SAY TO THE BLACK WOMAN?

Pro-Choice/Keep Abortion Legal Rally
The Mayflower Hotel, Washington D.C.
April 8, 1989

What is of use in these words I offer in memory and recognition of our common mother. And to my daughter.

What can the white man say to the black woman?

For four hundred years he ruled over the black woman's womb.

Let us be clear. In the barracoons and along the slave shipping coasts of Africa, for more than twenty generations, it was he who dashed our babies' brains out against the rocks.

What can the white man say to the black woman?

For four hundred years he determined which black woman's children would live or die.

Let it be remembered. It was he who placed our children on the auction block in cities all across the Eastern half of

442

what is now the United States, and listened to and watched them beg for their mothers' arms, before being sold to the highest bidder and dragged away.

What can the white man say to the black woman?

We remember that Fannie Lou Hamer, a poor sharecropper on a Mississippi plantation, was one of twenty-one children; and that on plantations across the South black women often had twelve, fifteen, twenty children. Like their enslaved mothers and grandmothers before them, these black women were sacrificed to the profit the white man could make from harnessing their bodies and their children's bodies to the cotton gin.

What can the white man say to the black woman?

We see him lined up, on Saturday nights, century after century, to make the black mother, who must sell her body to feed her children, go down on her knees to him.

Let us take note:

He has not cared for a single one of the dark children in his midst, over hundreds of years.

Where are the children of the Cherokee, my great-grandmother's people?
Gone.

Where are the children of the Blackfoot?
Gone.
Where are the children of the Lakota?
Gone.

Of the Cheyenne?
Of the Chippewa?
Of the Iroquois?
Of the Sioux?
Of the Akan?
Of the Ibo?
Of the Ashanti?
Of the Maori and the Aborigine?*

Where are the children of "the slave coast" and Wounded
Knee?

We do not forget the forced sterilizations and forced
starvations on the reservations, here as in South Africa. Nor
do we forget the smallpox-infested blankets Indian children
were given by the Great White Fathers of the United States
Government.

What has the white man to say to the black woman?

When we have children you do everything in your power
to make them feel unwanted from the moment they are

---

*Tribal, indigenous children destroyed during the white "settlement" of
the West.

born. You send them to fight and kill other dark mothers' children around the world. You shove them onto public highways into the path of oncoming cars. You shove their heads through plate glass windows. You string them up and you string them out.

What has the white man to say to the black woman?

From the beginning, you have treated all dark children with absolute hatred.

30,000,000 African children died on the way to the Americas, where nothing awaited them but endless toil and the crack of a bullwhip. They died of a lack of food, of lack of movement in the holds of ships. Of lack of friends and relatives. They died of depression, bewilderment and fear.

What has the white man to say to the black woman?

Let us look around us: Let us look at the world the white man has made for the black woman and her children.

It is a world in which the black woman is still forced to provide cheap labor, in the form of children, for the factory farms and on the assembly lines of the white man.

It is a world into which the white man dumps every foul, person-annulling drug he smuggles into Creation.

It is a world where many of our babies die at birth, or later of malnutrition, and where many more grow up to live lives of such misery they are forced to choose death by their own hands.

What has the white man to say to the black woman, and to all women and children everywhere?

Let us consider the depletion of the ozone; let us consider homelessness and the nuclear peril; let us consider the destruction of the rainforests—in the name of the almighty hamburger. Let us consider the poisoned apples and the poisoned water and the poisoned air, and the poisoned earth.

And that all of our children, because of the white man's assault on the planet, have a possibility of death by cancer in their almost immediate future.

What has the white male lawgiver to say to any of us? Those of us who love life too much to willingly bring more children into a world saturated with death.

Abortion, for many women, is more than an experience of suffering beyond anything most men will ever know, it is an act of mercy, and an act of self-defense.

To make abortion illegal, again, is to sentence millions of women and children to miserable lives and even more miserable deaths.

Given his history, in relation to us, I think the white man should be ashamed to attempt to speak for the unborn children of the black woman. To force us to have children for him to ridicule, drug, turn into killers and homeless wanderers is a testament to his hypocrisy.

What can the white man say to the black woman?

Only one thing that the black woman might hear.

Yes, indeed, the white man can say, your children have the right to life. Therefore I will call back from the dead those 30,000,000 who were tossed overboard during the centuries of the slave trade. And the other millions who died in my cotton fields and hanging from my trees.

I will recall all those who died of broken hearts and broken spirits, under the insult of segregation.

I will raise up all the mothers who died exhausted after birthing twenty-one children to work sunup to sundown on my plantation. I will restore to full health all those who perished for lack of food, shelter, sunlight, and love; and from my inability to recognize them as human beings.

But I will go even further:

I will tell you, black woman, that I wish to be forgiven the sins I commit daily against you and your children. For

I know that until I treat your children with love, I can never be trusted by my own. Nor can I respect myself.

And I will free your children from insultingly high infant mortality rates, short life spans, horrible housing, lack of food, rampant ill health. I will liberate them from the ghetto. I will open wide the doors of all the schools and the hospitals and businesses of society to your children. I will look at your children and see, not a threat, but a joy.

I will remove myself as an obstacle in the path that your children, against all odds, are making toward the light. I will not assassinate them for dreaming dreams and offering new visions of how to live. I will cease trying to lead your children, for I can see I have never understood where I was going. I will agree to sit quietly for a century or so, and meditate on this.

That is what the white man can say to the black woman.

We are listening.

ARMAH
OCTOBER 12, 1990

He came
in flowing robes
smelling
delicious.
My brother
from across the ocean.
My brother
from Africa.
How strong and slender
his body
feels
in my embrace.
How black and glowing
is his skin.
How warm
his eyes.
His is a beauty
I did not dare to dream
before I saw him.
I did not wish

to hurt
myself.

But now I sing
his beauty
both spirit
and body
my soul
content.

My brother looks
and speaks
and listens
the way
he writes.

It is heaven
to me
to see
the shape
of his lips
as he speaks
the curve of his
ear
as he listens
the eloquence of his palms
resting on the shoulders
of his sons.

To hear
the quiet rumble
of his voice.

My brother
has written books
that slayed my fear.

My brother
the writer
looks
and speaks
and listens
the way
he writes.

Now I have more
than his books
to love.

THE AWAKENING

for S.

When we met
we were already
friends.
Though I did not
know
who you were
or who
I was
at the time.
Me, old enough
to be your mother.
You
beautiful enough
to be
my son.
The how the why
the when of it
puzzles me.
As if middle age
which I neither
anticipated

nor feared
were merely
an opportunity
to redirect
one's way.
I long to watch
you sleep
in the night.
To find my new
self
awake
in your lightening dark
eyes
in the day.

A WOMAN IS NOT
A POTTED PLANT

her roots bound
to the confines
of her house

a woman is not
a potted plant
her leaves trimmed
to the contours
of her sex

a woman is not
a potted plant
her branches
espaliered
against the fences
of her race
her country
her mother
her man

her trained blossom
turning
this way
& that
to follow
the sun
of whoever feeds
and waters
her

a woman
is wilderness
unbounded
holding the future
between each breath
walking the earth
only because
she is free
and not creepervine
or tree.

Nor even honeysuckle
or bee.

The name "Lucy," which appears in the following poem, was given by paleoanthropologists to the fossilized skeleton of the most ancient, recognizably human being ever found. A woman who lived on the African continent some three million years ago.

WINNIE MANDELA
WE LOVE YOU

Winnie Mandela
We love you.

If we had known you
in a time of peace
we would have loved
your peacefulness
your quiet so deep
it did not hear
the call
to fight.

We missed our chance.

Winnie Mandela
We love you.

In a time of war
we love your ferocity.

We love your vigilance.
We love your impatience
with killers
and charlatans.
We love your hatred
of the deaths of our people.
We love your hatred
of despair.

Winnie Mandela
We love you.

We love your beauty.
We love your style.
We love your hats,
scarves
and various lengths
of hair.
We love the passion
in your body.
The fury in your eyes.
When you smile
we are amazed.

We love your loyalty
to Nelson
the beautiful.
Your attention to
the children
and the voluptuousness

of the countryside
which will be ours
again.
We love your memory
of details.
We love that you do not intend
to forget.

Winnie Mandela, "Lucy,"
We love you

for helping us recognize
the eternity
you've been with us before.

Winnie Mandela, Sister,
We love you.

Yours is the contemporary face
of the mother
of the human race.

WE HAVE A
BEAUTIFUL MOTHER

We have a beautiful
mother
Her hills
are buffaloes
Her buffaloes
hills.

We have a beautiful
mother
Her oceans
are wombs
Her wombs
oceans.

We have a beautiful
mother
Her teeth
the white stones
at the edge
of the water

the summer
grasses
her plentiful
hair.

We have a beautiful
mother
Her green lap
immense
Her brown embrace
eternal
Her blue body
everything
we know.

ONCE, AGAIN

Once again simple
Once again childlike
The poem opening out
into the grass.